DAUGHTER

DAUGHTER

The Soul Journey of a Black Woman in America
Having a Human Experience

EBONEE DAVIS

Andrews McMeel
PUBLISHING®

Andrews McMeel Publishing
a division of Andrews McMeel Universal
1130 Walnut Street, Kansas City, Missouri 64106

www.andrewsmcmeel.com

23 24 25 26 27 SDB 10 9 8 7 6 5 4 3 2 1

ISBN: 978-1-5248-8135-1

Library of Congress Control Number: 2023934439

Editor: Danys Mares
Art Director/Designer: Tiffany Meairs
Production Editor: Margaret Utz
Production Manager: Shona Burns

Illustration by Deun Ivory

DISCLAIMER: Some names and identifying characteristics
have been changed to protect the privacy of the individuals
involved.

"Time For Change" was previously published in a different form
in *Harper's Bazaar*, July 2016.

ATTENTION: SCHOOLS AND BUSINESSES
Andrews McMeel books are available at quantity discounts with
bulk purchase for educational, business, or sales promotional use.
For information, please e-mail the Andrews McMeel Publishing
Special Sales Department: sales@amuniversal.com.

For my nephews.
May the world you grow up in be a better place
because of it.

Preface

I often find myself gazing out at the trees just beyond my living room window as they wave their branches and greet each new dawn with grace and fortitude. I watch as they change day by day, surrendering to the season—to the wind and the rain, to the heat and the cold, to the storms and the snow. Through it all, their roots remain firmly planted. Come spring, I admire the cherry blossoms and the bees they entice. Come summer, I admire the vibrant green leaves. Come fall, I admire the rich, warm hues of red, yellow, and orange. Come winter, I admire the space that is created for this cycle to take place all over again the following year.

It is necessary for the trees to lose their leaves each winter so that they can return even more magnificent than before. With each season, their trunks widen and their roots deepen. And because we understand this cyclical shedding and blooming, we never think to ourselves, "This tree is dying." We understand that it is part of a process, and we perceive this shedding and clearing-away of the old as preparation for what is to come, rather than as an ending. Every time the trees surrender and shed, they are given an opportunity to add.

With this analogy in mind, I invite you to consider for a moment that perhaps the way we have agreed to regard death in the Western world may very well be a misinterpretation of the truth: Death is not the antithesis of life but rather the catalyst for it. Death is the very function that ensures life's continuation. It is the eternal tango between life and death that perpetuates the fundamental experience of existence on Earth: evolution. And it is one's ability to adapt that dictates the quality of this experience.

The evidence of this relationship is all around us and we can observe this dance in patterns throughout nature. The caterpillar begins its life belly to the ground, limited to its immediate surroundings, vision obstructed by all that grows tall around it. The caterpillar assumes that this form is the sum of its being, unaware of what it has yet to become. It does not know that the mundanity of its present existence pales in comparison to the life it is destined to live.

Then the caterpillar is called, just as we are called, to abandon this form and become something greater. But in order to undergo this great transformation, the caterpillar must retreat into the darkness and solitude of its own chrysalis. It must face a small "death." Not of the flesh or the spirit but of the mind, which has assumed an identity based on the caterpillar's past experiences. The mind only knows that which has been—unlike the soul, which holds the codes to our ascensions before we are even birthed into this physical dimension—and cannot conceive of that which has yet to come.

After this period of "death" and darkness, the butterfly emerges, wings to the sky. Its world changes, not because it demands anything outside of itself to change, but because the butterfly surrendered to its pending evolution. It released all attachments to the life it had known, allowing its own perspective to shift. When the butterfly changed itself, it changed its entire reality.

The butterfly demonstrates for us that our culturally agreed upon notions of death are false: Death is not a bleak and final farewell that we must dread but a gateway to a new evolutionary beginning. It is not something to run from or mourn over. It is perhaps even a cause for celebration. Death is not an ending but a reentering of the womb, so that we may be further gestated and birthed once more into a higher dimension of our being. It is not separate from life but a phase in life's cyclical unfolding. Not only is it essential, but death, like birth, is one of life's most sacred processes; it is the harmonious union of life and death that allows our very existence to be renewed, reshaped, and reimagined.

Like butterflies, we are born first to our biological mothers, and years later, after having lived out our adolescence bound by the limitations and expectations of our environment, identities shaped entirely by the programming of our families, the culture into which we were born, and the ideas we have of ourselves bound by others' imaginative constructs, we are called to reenter the womb of the cosmic mother so that we may be born again. This is the hero's journey, a story template common across civilizations all throughout history. Odysseus, for example, set sail for ten years and faced a number of trials before returning home to meet his highest calling and defeat the suitors who had taken possession of his land in his absence. Or Simba, the young cub in *The Lion King* who runs away from home tormented by the belief that he is responsible for his father's death. With the help of some unlikely allies and a series of initiations that transform Simba from cub to king, he returns to Pride Rock to claim his throne and cast out the reigning evil.

The word "hero" itself may be misleading, as it alludes to glamour and excitement, but for a true hero, the transformation from mundane to supernatural is often characterized by feelings of fear, anger, resentment, and sadness as they are forced to leave their family and community behind in search of an identity outside the binding social contracts of culture and tradition. The journey is not easy but, as in all of creation, the most beautiful life-forms frequently rise from the most adverse conditions, such as the lotus flower from mud or the rose from concrete. Perhaps with these metaphorical symbols of our own potential for transformation at hand, we can learn to use our energy to nurture who we are becoming rather than desperately grasping the past.

The sacred scarab, also known as the dung beetle, depicted throughout ancient Egyptian art, is another example of the dance between life and death. It is born into a pile of feces upon which it feasts until it becomes aware of its wings and makes its departure. It is the very thing that nourishes and protects the dung beetle in its infancy which limits its full potential as it matures. The dung beetle must abandon its place of birth if it wishes to live an exceedingly better life. As with the dung beetle, it is often the very thing that sustains us in our infancy and adolescence that hinders us from reaching our full potential in adulthood. If we sit upon the pile of dung we were born into long enough, we cease to smell it. From our families and communities we learn ways of being that are essential to our survival within those contexts and may yield moderate success but ultimately become destructive or limiting elsewhere. Quite often we remain unaware of the pile of shit upon which we have built our lives and our familiarity with it keeps us stagnant. We choose it over and over, not because it is what we truly desire, but because we know how to function within it and therefore it presents an element of safety. It is our work to go within ourselves to find out who we truly are, beyond the limitations of the mind that knows only where and what we have been, so that we may ascend beyond the parameters of our past like the butterfly and the sacred scarab.

Our greatest gift as human beings, and the characteristic that separates us from the natural world and animal kingdom, is our ability to choose our becoming. We as humans have the unique capacity to take part in our own evolution. If we can learn to dance with death rather than classify it as something to be feared, we can also learn to welcome life's changes knowing that everything is unfolding for our highest good, even when we find ourselves in a state of discomfort. In this way, we alleviate our own suffering by detaching from expectations of how things should be or memories of how things have been, creating space for new and wonderful possibilities.

She Is Coming

I wonder if trees watch the moon
And know when to ask for fruit
Do they long for June
When January makes a mockery
Of last season's creations?
Or do they know
January is preparing them
For something greater?
Do they understand cycles?
Because if I did,
Instead of holding on
I might just let go
I might live in the present
Because although I don't
Fear the future,
I'm aware of its
Ebb and flow
But I wouldn't cherish
One over the other,
I'd know they're both necessary
Like stubbed toes
Teach us as children not to cut corners
We don't always listen
But the signs are always there
I wonder if as a child I knew my pain was preparing me for more
I never let it swallow me whole

Not the same way it swallowed
Everyone around me
My mother
My sister
My friends
My community

I became a cavity
In the mouth of the beast
Because I stayed too sweet
Like the day I was born
My grandma used to call me
A little chocolate drop
Maybe that's what she mean
She was always clairvoyant
And that's how I learned to see
Maybe her words were prophecy
I was here to rot the system
The dentures
That clenched down
On centuries of women
Preventing them from
Knowing the truth
In this dimension
We rule and our wisdom
Comes from the womb
We've been given
Our connection to God

Has been pillaged
Like the land we descend from

Who is defending the land I descend from?

Deafening screams
Deferred dreams
Diluted streams
So apparently no one

SOLD to the highest bidder
Don't ask me why I'm bitter
I've tasted bloody rivers
Wounds stung by salt water
When human cargo gets delivered
I've had my womb raided
My children taken and
My body drilled in
Build the skyscraper
But burn down the village
Love the oil
But hate human of the same pigment
Bottom of the ship
Not a single pot to piss in
Rob the land of its riches
Then paint depictions of sickness
Breast-fed liquid gold
Whole world latched on my titty

Such a pity they
Let me die in labor
Still use my sons
To build their cities
Private prisons
Electoral committees
The auction block a courtroom
Souls bought and sold for pennies

Parasitic blood suckers
Sadistic motherfuckers
Genocidal gun lovers

Invading territory
We hold sacred
Our grandmothers' psyches
Hold enough secrets
To sink spaceships
Heavy is the head that wears the crown,
They say the kitchen's
Where the nape is
Probably because these crops
Fed a whole nation
My cornrows and my cajun
Still got brothers caged in
My caviar, my Black skin
Thirty-one flavors to bask in
Robbed of second chances

Turn a mattress to a casket

Who is defending the land I descend from?

Deafening screams
Deferred dreams
Diluted streams
So apparently no one

SOLD to the loneliest sinner
My heartbeat
My center
Broke me every time they'd enter
Worth her weight in gold
My mother's body dismembered
Watched her give pieces
To men like oaks
Give leaves to the ground
In September
I'd rake up every one
For her just to remember
Dull every axe
That left limbs splintered
Re-member
She is my timber
And I am the sweet fruit
Brought to fruition
Through friction, rain, sunshine,

And resilience
My pit will be
My legacy
And the proof
Of my healing
Achilles tendon
Shackled feet
My soul cries out for centuries of the feminine
Indigenous rhythms
Silenced by systems
Scales of justice more poisonous
Than rattlesnake venom
Since infancy we're given
Substandard living
Subverted narratives
And subsequent syndromes
Food in the fridge and
Heat where we living
And lights for the children
All brought to you by
Nights at the Hilton
And tears that were hidden

Patterns of detachment
And subjugated feelings
Shame that you live with
Ignoring all the whispers
Sunday morning baptisms

And conjugal kisses
Silk pressed salon trips n'
Abortion clinic visits
Rest never given
Rest never given

Who is defending the land I descend from?

Deafening screams
Deferred dreams
Diluted streams
So apparently no one

SOLD colonial dreams
So it seems
They not for me
Four hundred years of sowing seeds
Harvest season
This time I reap
Say a prayer
Lay them down to sleep
Take up arms
Don't forget
Crown and feet

That's God Body
Their design to destroy
But forgot about the God in me

Voice like alchemy
Tongue like sword
Slice through fallacy
Ready the blade
Machete swings

Who is defending the land I descend from?

Am I the only one
Aware of the truth
Or the only one
Not pretending

Many moons
Many women
Many children
They are coming
You can feel them

The hurricanes, the flood,
The buzz, the bees,
The earthquakes, the droughts,
The famine, the disease
Out of the darkness born
Light embodied
She is coming and
She is me

Origin

eboree

lola

grandpa larry

mom

laci

Circles

Go in circles like cursive

Breaking curses
I'm immersed in the challenge
Of becoming my own person

I often flirt with higher versions
But still I'm unlearning
That which I was birthed in

Shed my leaves
Take the fall
Surrender to seasons
They serve to evolve

Nana

My grandmother, "Nana," Nancy Carol Palmer by birth, chanted for me the way a Southern Baptist grandmother prays for her grandchild. She converted to Buddhism because she "never felt imaginative enough" to create the life she wanted for herself. She says chanting endowed her with the necessary faith and practices for envisioning and cultivating a more fulfilling life. I remember attending the SGI Community Center with Nana as a child and chanting "nam my oho renge kyo" in a room full of hundreds as the vibration from those ancient words rippled through my body. Both of my grandmothers were Buddhist, so it was not unlikely that when attending the community center with one, I might run into the other, or into some friend of the family. Although she was born in Pendleton, Oregon, Nana's Houston, Texas, roots, like most Black Americans of that time, meant she was raised Christian. But, in the fifth grade, she "converted" to Catholicism because Catholic schools provided the best education.

Nana's schooling was paid for by her father, my great-grandfather, Arthur James "Bantu" Palmer Sr. Bantu was a self-given middle name that signified his connection to Bantuism, the religion he practiced which rooted itself in African traditionalism. However, most simply knew him as "Big Daddy." An entrepreneur and activist to most and a rebel to some, he hailed from DeFuniak, Florida, the third child of nine. DeFuniak was a dangerous place for a Black man to be in the 1930s, so when he was sixteen, although still underage, he went chasing after his older brother, who had joined the military two years prior. Big Daddy traveled around the country, got married, had children, and ended a marriage and began another one all before settling in Portland, Oregon, where he lived out the remainder of his life before passing in 2013.

* * *

The first Black-owned motel in Portland belonged to Big Daddy. So did another motel, a hotel, two apartment buildings, and a grocery store. The laundromat, hair salon, and corner store he owned all sat connected on the same block. Tina, my youngest brother's mother, worked at the hair salon, which is how she and my father met. He enticed her with the fried chicken he made daily in the corner store's kitchen. Working in my great-grandfather's corner store is the job my father worked "between jobs." He also worked for Big Daddy's tow truck company and in the office of his taxi company, Rose City Cab. I remember sitting on my father's lap as a small child, using the radio to dispatch drivers to their pick-up locations.

I did a research project on Big Daddy in elementary school and learned that he was responsible in part for desegregating the Portland waterfront and creating opportunities for Black workers to find employment on the docks. I also learned that at one point he ran for city council and was closely affiliated with American politicians and change makers of the highest ranks, including John F. Kennedy. He ran Kennedy's election campaign in Portland and even got him to give a speech at my grandmother's Catholic school. This was not surprising to learn because this was the version of my great-grandfather that I experienced daily. I only knew the well-dressed man who picked me up from school in his long champagne-colored

Cadillac and took me to Popeyes for a chicken and a biscuit and took me to run errands with him until my dad got off work. I only knew the man who held "Redemption Hour" in the home next to his (which he also owned but used as a halfway house for those in need). Every Sunday, friends, family, and community members all crowded into the living room of that house and sat in rows of odd chairs to hear his message. The homeless and addicted were especially welcomed, and he'd preach the importance of our ancestral connection and make sure that we knew our people originated from Angola, Africa. I only knew—and absolutely loved—the charisma, the charm, and the benevolence of Big Daddy.

As his name implies, he sat at the helm of our family—he was the glue that kept intact not only us but the entire neighborhood. He supplied jobs, gave advice, and offered shelter to anyone who asked, including my father, who lived in his basement after completing his rehab program. Some of my earliest memories of my dad are visiting him while he lived in that basement, and, because of this, Big Daddy's house will forever be etched into my memory. The huge tree out back and the grapevines that gave us delicious fruit every summer. The bathroom walls that had been completely covered in shaggy material, cut and collaged together to create an image of the night sky. The old walnuts that sat in thick pink and blue crystal dishes on the coffee table in the living room. The cream-colored sofa that was never taken out of its plastic and the thick plastic runners that covered the floor. It was kept as more of a museum than a living room. Most of the living took place in the den; I remember that space with such clarity. The dim lighting and wood-paneled walls. The Black figurines that sat on a small table near the window. The paintings of African women wearing neck-elongating jewelry. The recliner Big Daddy sat in. The massive, big-screen television. And the door that lead to my favorite room: the kitchen.

* * *

In the kitchen, I would sit at the tiled counter in a wooden chair that was bolted to the floor and rotated back and forth while my great-grandmother Anita fixed me breakfast. Her cocker spaniel Toby would play at my feet and keep me company as I sat waiting for the food. My great-grandmother was sweet with an unmistakably high-pitched voice. Every once in a while she'd use that voice to tell me to stop spinning in the chair, because the arms of it would hit the countertop, which eventually caused the wood to begin chipping. My great-grandmother Anita, "Grandma Nita" for short, loved everybody deeply, and I believe the source of this love was the love she had first for herself. The beauty she brought into the world and offered us flowed first through her vessel and then on to others. Her hair was always pulled back neat into a French roll. Her long round fingernails were always polished pink, never chipped or uneven. Her clothes were always ironed, and her lips were always painted. Grandma Nita also had her own house just minutes down the road from Big Daddy's. It was white on the outside and pink on the inside like a Barbie playhouse. Nothing in her life was any less fabulous than that, and this extraordinary level of self-care was reflected in how she treated others. She was the type who gave everybody around her a nickname based on their own special relationship, not on what anybody else called them. My sister was "Bites" because as a baby she'd yell, "Bites! Bites! Bites!" whenever she was hungry . . . and that was often. For a short time, I lived with Grandma Nita, because my father left town for reasons I can't remember. She curated an experience of beauty and femininity that remains with me to this day. Her home was full of polish and perfume and all the things you would expect of a true lady and none of the things I had access to living with my father. I received news of her passing while standing in a crowded New York subway, headed home one evening while I was living there and working as a model. I sobbed quietly as strangers handed me tissue and held space for my grief.

Although she was married to my great-grandfather long before I was born, Grandma Nita was not my biological great-grandmother. My great-grandmother Eddie Lee Burns, Grandma Eddie for short, passed away from a brain hemorrhage one year after I was born. I don't have any memories of my own, only a few photographs and the stories I've been told. My dad tells me she was a great cook, and my Nana describes her as a "kind of princess." Her father, Edward Burns, owned a successful mechanic business in the South so she never wanted for much. She met Big Daddy while visiting her uncle in California in her early twenties and, legend has it, she would not have sex with him until they were married. Nana thinks they had sex but that Big Daddy kept his word and flew her to Mexico to get married first. After Grandma Eddie got pregnant with the couple's first child, she moved back to her hometown of Houston, Texas, to be close to her family. That is where she gave birth to Arthur Jr. In those days, it was customary for a woman to be near her mother when bearing and raising small children. But, regardless of the distance, she remained married to my great-grandfather. Two years later, she gave birth to my grandmother, Nancy Carol Palmer, in Pendleton, Oregon.

The marriage only lasted five years, so by the time Nana was two, Grandma Eddie had once again returned to Houston. Nana lived there with Grandma Eddie until she was about ten years old. She tells me that *her* grandmother, "Big Mama," was a midwife and that every Sunday she would gather the family and cook fried chicken for everybody. Just as Nana was about to enter the fifth grade, her mother decided to send her and her brother to Portland, Oregon, where Big Daddy had put down roots. I am not clear on the time in between, but from what I have been told, my great-grandmother Eddie eventually ended up living in New York City during the latter part of her life. After living there seven years myself, I grew fond of the idea that perhaps some of the footsteps I took on that pavement were also taken by her.

According to Nana, Arthur Jr. was my great-grandmother's pride and joy. He was a very good-looking young man with fair skin and silky hair, which meant a great deal back then. She was darker with kinkier hair and never felt as admired. Arthur Jr. grew into quite the ladies' man, having seven kids and four wives by the time of his passing at age thirty-five. Even though she was almost certain Arthur Jr. received more love from their parents, this did not change the love Nana felt for him. They looked after one another. Their father wouldn't have it any other way. In grade school, he fought her bullies and protected her as she walked home. They were close this way up until Arthur Jr.'s passing. The autopsy ruled that he died of an accidental overdose, though Big Daddy never accepted this as the truth. He maintained that Arthur Jr. died from a respiratory condition that runs in the family.

Although the truth of Arthur Jr.'s death is somewhat of a mystery, what I know for sure is that only a year after he and his sister were sent to live with their father, newspapers began publishing vicious stories that vilified Big Daddy. They painted him as a criminal and accused him of buying property with money gained from trafficking cocaine. For the most part, the headlines were right. In addition to business ownership and activism, my great-grandfather participated in some alternative entrepreneurial ventures that eventually led to his arrest and the seizure of most of his properties. Because of his position in the community, Big Daddy's arrest sent shockwaves through the press. It was this series of events that eventually led to Big Daddy's falling out with John F. Kennedy. Kennedy did not want to be affiliated with the drug business and thought it best to cut ties. According to my grandmother, my great-grandfather "cursed him out," arguing that the Kennedys themselves had acquired their wealth from selling alcohol during Prohibition. He asserted that this was no different and the only thing that made him a target was the color of his skin. Kennedy did not take this well and the two went their separate ways. Just months before the election, and after running Kennedy's local campaign office, Big Daddy gave his endorsement to Nixon.

My grandmother says that this time caused her a lot of embarrassment and that everybody knew she was the daughter of a "thug." I can only imagine how hurtful and confusing it must have been then to lose a brother twenty years later to that very same substance and then to nearly lose a son.

* * *

My grandmother wore an afro like mine in the '70s. At that time, she had a wide gap in the front of her mouth but got it filled before I was born. My father's gap appears more and more as he ages. I often wonder if one day I will inherit this trait as well. The scar above my left eye is from my grandmother's cat, Chloe, who clawed me for continuing to provoke her after she no longer wanted to play—perhaps my earliest lesson in consent. During the summer months, which I spent in Seattle with my mom, Nana would pick me up with jazz playing softly in the car. Always jazz, nothing else. To this day that's all I've ever known her to listen to. She brought me around her friends quite often. They were a circle of successful Black people who had done well for themselves by following the equation that society gives us to achieve success: Education equals opportunity. Although we have seen in recent years that this was never a sustainable model for growth and our success isn't always contingent upon how hard we study, she made it through college with two children and got a job that was able to sustain her and provide a comfortable life. She worked the same job for thirty years and drove the same car for thirteen—a navy blue Infiniti with tan leather interior. I still remember the way the leather smelled and how it began cracking in the place where she rested her right elbow as she drove. Every day she pulled in and out of her driveway on Alder Street in the Central

District of Seattle, Washington, and drove downtown, where she worked as a budget analyst for the city. And although this meant that she and her friends sometimes bonded over bootstrap rhetoric because they believed themselves to be living proof of the American Dream, they had certainly created something for themselves. Many of them the first generation to not just survive but thrive since their ancestors were brought over in chains. They partied and went on ski trips and camping excursions, and Nana took me along. I witnessed them and their poise, those Black folk who seemed to have it together in a way that I did not see in my everyday life. As a child, I found it terribly dull, but as an adult I am clear on Nana's intention and so I am grateful.

Nana, like most grandparents, wanted me to have a life different from the one she had growing up and the one I was destined for if left only to the care of my parents. So she took me with her whenever and wherever she could. She still reminds me of our trip to Disneyland and how if I was not riding the roller coaster, I was at the hotel pool, and how on our trip to Jamaica I would not get out of the ocean. Her absolute favorite story to tell is of the evening I spent the night at her house and was prepared for bed, bonnet and all, but could not find my Barbie pajamas. No more than four years of age and knee high to a grasshopper, I stood with my arms folded in protest, accusing her of misplacing them, which she found hysterical. The next morning, I walked up to her, pajamas in hand, after finding them tucked down into the side of my bed, which was met with even more laughter. My grandmother loved me then and still refers to me now as her "most favorite person in the world." That is a statement I never questioned, although this love, given from someone who lost so much so early, has sometimes taken on the shape of fear.

You Are

You are your ancestors' good karma.

You are the twinkle in every eye left puffy and red from crying.

You are 70 percent water, and 100 percent of that is composed of the sweat and tears shed by your kinfolk.

You are a soft touch from hands made callous by hard work.

You are every lash on their backs, every lash on their lids, and every hair on your head was prayed over a thousand times before you were born.

You are the terrified women in your lineage who said yes to life despite their fears and hesitations.

You are the answer to those who questioned their capacity to raise a child under less than ideal circumstances.

You are the personification of a commitment to surviving and making it look beautiful.

You are Grandma's pearls.

You are the family heirloom held sacred and handed down from generation to generation.

You are every tongue rejoicing and every hallelujah sang from lips.

You are the ritual, the river, the Bible, and the baptism.

You are Mama's baby.

You are what was manifested when a body became a portal to usher in new life.

You are the result of a heart summoned by the Most High and an act of surrender.

You are chains broken.

You are the end of one cycle and the beginning of another.

You are the steps taken away from what in your past has not honored you.

You are the bridges burned that put distance between you and what did not set your soul on fire.

You are the ashes remaining from expired versions of yourself.

You are fertile ground.

You are rain on cracked land after seasons of drought.

You are the feast to a malnourished vessel after centuries of being
fed only crumbs.

You are pound cake made from scratch using a handwritten recipe
after decades of sugar-coated lies.

You are a cool beverage on a hot day finally washing down a
reality that has been hard to swallow.

You are generational wealth.

You are the divine inheritance your descendants are waiting on.

You are all that has been and all that will be summed up into one
lifetime of opportunity.

You are the past, present, and future.

You are the seed and the harvest.

You are the soil and the garden.

You are your ancestors' good karma.

Lala

When thinking of my grandmother Lala, I, like many others when reflecting on memories of their family's maternal backbone, first think of her kitchen. I think of the basket of onions and garlic that hung above her sink. I think of her refrigerator, which she kept full of fruits and vegetables for visits from grandchildren, and the butter tubs that often contained anything but butter: leftover spaghetti, oatmeal, baked chicken. I think of the cabinets full of tea and snacks and an assortment of Chinese herbal medicine and candy that she administered whenever one of us felt even the slightest bit ill. I think of the compost container that, when full of eggshells and coffee grounds and other food scraps, we would dump into her small garden out back where she grew potatoes. I think of the strawberry bushes and cherry trees just outside the window whose fruit didn't stand a chance against me, my sister, and my cousins. And I especially think of her collection of wooden spoons that sat on the counter by the cutting board. Spoons of all shapes and sizes, some round, some square, some with thick, flat handles, some with skinny cylindrical ones. Those spoons set our backsides on fire when we acted out of line but also kept us fed, especially when our mother could not.

* * *

Betty Lu Cottrell was born in 1939 amid the Great Depression. She speaks of rural Saskatchewan, her birthplace, where most farmed and lived uneventful lives. She speaks of being raised by her Ukrainian grandmother while her mother chased employment. She speaks of being so poor that it was not uncommon to eat only lard on bread and for the boys she walked past on her way to school to call her names like "beanpole." After all, she stood 5'10" with thick, dark hair and penetrating blue eyes that made obvious the freezing climate from which her ancestors originated. She speaks of meeting her father only once—an Englishman and war veteran who was held as a POW in WWII. She speaks of seeing him pursue her aunt in that short window of time when he existed beyond the parameters of her imagination. How uncomfortable it must have been to witness this as a young girl who, like all young girls, conscious of it or not, want to be wanted by their fathers and will spend their lifetime searching for this love if not received early on. She speaks of her aunt who raised her sister. And she speaks of witnessing death, both of body and spirit—the death that is invited in by a lifetime of compromise. She speaks of her sister passing from leukemia at age twelve and her grandmother soon after. She speaks of once again living with her mother, who married and moved in with the man whose house she cleaned and how from this union she gained two step-siblings and a half-brother.

My Canadian grandmother did not see a Black person until she was fifteen years old but eventually moved across the border from Vancouver, British Columbia, to Seattle, Washington, to marry my Black American grandfather, a St. Louis native. She brought with her my Aunt Bernadine and my Aunt Brenda, both born from a previous marriage. She also brought with her my Uncle Michael, the son they had together, who was just an infant at the time. After my grandfather finished his stint in the Navy, the couple moved in together and my mother was born. To this day, my grandmother still lives in that very same house, though, due to the internal battles life has enlisted her in, it looks a lot different now. My grandfather

Lonnie Marcus Visor, nicknamed "Larry" in the Navy, was tall and wide with small freckles and moles all over his face and neck. I have recently started to notice them on myself. I did not know him well because he and my grandmother were divorced by the time I was born, but I do remember the trip on which he took my cousin Jordan (Michael's son), my sister, and me to Wild Waves Amusement Park. He chain-smoked with the windows up the entire forty-five-minute drive there and his voice sounded like every last cigarette he smoked. My mother doesn't have much to say about his dreams or aspirations when I ask, only that he liked lotto tickets and white women. She says this with a smile.

My grandma recalls clearly what it was like dating a Black man in the '70s, particularly the racial slurs, like "nigger lover," constantly hurled by strangers. It was a hate she did not understand. She recalls this hate infiltrating her family and how my mother found it particularly difficult to navigate conflicting and complex identities growing up biracial. She remembers my mother being filled with rage because of it, and this rage she would often take out on my grandmother. She believes this rage may have been the source of the emotional pain that drove my mother to addiction.

She speaks of this very matter-of-factly when I ask questions about her past. It is evident that my grandmother embodied resilience, not as a matter of seeking human nobility or even intentionally but as a means of survival. She was tough. She cursed like a sailor, which made sense because she worked on Seattle's waterfront as a longshoreman. One of the few women down there doing "man's work." She became restless when she couldn't use her body to perform labor in this way. She'd take me down to the docks with her often during my elementary and middle school summers in Seattle. It was there, among those brawny men, that I learned how to play gin rummy and other gambling games. I played cards throughout the day with my grandmother at her dining room table, so, down at the docks, I won more often than one might expect from a child. I loved being treated like an adult, like someone with a worldview all their own. I loved the conversations we had in the morning. She'd serve me coffee with cream and nearly-burnt buttered toast and we'd talk, not about childish things but about things like politics, war, and what was going on with the economy.

Growing up I believed my grandmother was rich, though she still preferred to hang clothes out on the line to dry in the backyard rather than using the machine. And even on the coldest winter day, with the ground covered in a thick white blanket of snow, my grandmother was still reluctant to turn on the heat. Instead, she dressed warmly, adding on extra layers of clothing, and urged us to do the same. "Grab a pair of wool socks" was her verbal offering to me, and she had plenty because the temperature fell below freezing often down on the waterfront and her work required stiff steel-toe boots. On days where I would make it back home from school before she returned from work, I'd crank the thermostat up to 80 degrees and sit in front of the vent until she got home. When I heard her car pulling up, I'd quickly rush to turn it off.

Although her days as a longshoreman provided her with enough to rescue us in times of need, I know now that the reason for my belief in my grandmother's affluence was her spirit, which overflowed with abundance. Life's simple pleasures were her beacon, moving her toward hope even in times of deep sadness. I could always call on her to come pick me up when my mom hadn't fed me or my sister was terrorizing me. Because of this, I knew her number by heart by the age of four. We'd walk around her neighborhood every evening sifting through garage sales, rummaging through the recently discarded items that sat in front of Goodwill prior to intake, visiting thrift shops and stopping to indulge in the edible plants that grew wild in the cracks of the sidewalks. She enjoyed things that only nature could supply. She'd take my sister and me to Green Lake and let us swim for hours on end and then we'd swing on the playground and she'd push us while we shouted, "To the moon, Lala! To the moon!" We called her Lala because she sang to us in a voice that was sweet like maple syrup and, as babies of a mother who could hardly see past her own pain long enough to acknowledge ours, we yearned for this simple pleasure. She turned going to the food bank into an adventure, which was much more exciting than going to a regular grocery store, because finding produce that hadn't yet expired felt like striking gold. Whenever we'd ask her to, she'd rub our backs and massage the tension from our bodies—even as a child I held so much in my shoulders that went unexpressed. But I felt everything, and my grandmother knew it. When I was six or seven, she told me I was different, and that I chose my parents so I could grow strong from the experience. This sentiment gave context to my feelings of otherness; it provided an explanation for why I seemed to view the world so differently from my parents and siblings. At a young age, I witnessed with clarity the energy and intention behind people's words and often misaligned actions, and I did not understand why so often the adults in my life seemed to lack this same understanding. I saw their unspoken truths and she saw mine.

Recipes

My father gave me recipes
Collard greens
Mac n cheese
He gave me survival
By any means
He gave me candied yams
Despite
Black-eyed dreams

Father
Part One

My dad's deep baritone voice will carry on, vibrating through the corridors of my mind, the ones which house the most precious memories from my childhood, long after his body has vanished.

When he spoke, it was like rain. Calm, soothing. And when he yelled it was like thunder. Booming, abrupt. Percussion meant everything to my father. Grooves and rhythms worked well for him. Routines, structure, discipline. A true creature of habit, for better or for worse, with a strange proclivity for collecting things that should have been thrown out right away—nail clippings, sunflower seeds, beer cans. He kept these things in small piles adjacent to his alarm clock and answering machine on the dark walnut side table next to his bed, which he covered with a forest green hand towel. Although he was unaware of it at the time, this was his altar. There he placed the things he valued.

My father ate Cheerios or Frosted Flakes every morning for breakfast, except on days when he cooked for the family or I took the liberty of doing so. Luckily for us, he loved cooking and did so whenever he could, which was sometimes impossible because of his work schedule and how tired he was. On weekends and days when work did not require him to leave the house before I woke for school, I'd be lured downstairs by the smell of bacon cooking in the oven. I'd eat and watch back-to-back videos on VH1 Soul, which constantly streamed throughout our home. To this day he aspires to operate a food truck and write a recipe book, though in recent years life has forced him into the role of a sanitation worker. I learned from him how easily you can let yourself be destroyed if you are not vigilant.

* * *

While visiting my father in Atlanta in 2017, I remember him saying something about not being able to sing. It was not as if his voice had fallen out or that it had changed, it was simply that his belief in it was gone. I found this quite shocking, as many of my most cherished childhood memories involve hearing my dad's voice filling the space around me on long car rides to the beach or cruising up I-5 as I sat in the back seat and absorbed the bass rattling through my small body. In that moment, I hurt for my father; I became aware that he had been robbed of something I was certain could not be taken away. Maybe growing older had something to do with it, but I know for sure that the greatest reason was that his soul had been siphoned out of him. My father is an example of what I mean when I talk about our divinity being systematically forced out of us. It is impossible to explain the pain of seeing him go from the vibrant and free man of my youth to someone who makes compromises for the survival of his vessel with complete disregard for the survival of his soul.

From what he has shared with me, I know that he felt the same way I did growing up: well-known but never popular. And I know that he wanted to be somebody. Or rather, that he already sensed he was somebody and simply needed a chance to show it. He still remembers hearing "Rapper's Delight" for the first time on the radio and how he ran to the boom box in disbelief to turn it up. He remembers singing and dancing in Bubbling Brown Sugar, Seattle's city-wide talent competition, and how the ladies referred to him as Chocolate Charm thereafter. He says this with a toothy grin, and it all makes sense.

For as far back as I can remember, music was my father's therapy, his confidant, his best friend. I remember posters of 2Pac and Janet Jackson on the wall in my great-grandfather's basement where I'd visit my father after he finished rehab. Then, when we got our home, I remember my father building his CD collection in the hallway just outside his bedroom. Hundreds of CDs stacked upon one another in no particular order. I get my poetry and my sensitivity from my father. Sensitivity that, for him, could only be expressed, heard, and felt through music.

I remember the droplets of rain that pooled on the windows of my father's car and reflected the streetlights as he drove home one stormy evening. I can't remember where he'd picked me up from, but what I do remember is him turning around to face me in the back seat and apologizing. He explained that he was in a bad mood and needed to listen to something with some curse words in it. I understood then that his emotions were always made obvious by the music he was listening to. I knew when I was in trouble, when all was well, when he had a hard day at work, when things were going his way, and even when he felt close to God—during those times he listened to a lot of Gospel. He allowed the lyrics of his favorite artists to vent for him, demand justice for him, celebrate for him, give thanks for him, and express what he could not—feelings that so often went unacknowledged. I would not say that my father was an angry person, but rather that anger lived inside of him, only needing minimal provocation to be brought forth. His particular genre of anger was rooted in sadness and loss, emotions too long ignored and made abnormal by the expectations of a patriarchal society. So he turned his car into a sanctuary and rocked his head to music to quell the storm that raged inside of him.

* * *

Upon relocating to Atlanta last year, I stayed with my dad for a couple of weeks while I searched for a place to live. For the first time in seventeen years, I was once again sharing space with the man who attended every middle school dance recital and still regrets missing one. The man who redecorated my room while I was away for the summer to celebrate my matriculation into the sixth grade. The man who came to my rescue and sat in the principal's office demanding justice after bullies at school threw chocolate milk on me, staining my clothes. And the man who life ripped me away from, with whom my relationship would take over a decade to repair. On my first day in town, I got in an Uber outside of his home, which drove to the end of the block before turning, heading in the direction of my destination. I noticed then that the end of the block was a cul-de-sac exactly like the one he and I lived on together in Portland. In that moment, I felt God smiling down on me, reminding me that all things come full circle. I knew instantly that I was in a season of restoration, that God was placing us back into perfect alignment.

Eye

I just want the right to remain
You can save what comes after
Want my existence
My laughter
My success and
My past hurt
To be enough so my mama
Not in front of a pastor
Asking her God "WHY!!"
Ain't that shit backward?
How we get labeled criminal
Abducted
No passport

A toe tag
A man's worth
My hands hurt
Blistered
Holding up
This system
Common sense is canceled
Dying under capitalism
How long we gonna act like the structure
Ain't the sickness
Like the stress from that man's work
Ain't send him home quicker

Which curse is worse - the fast food
Or the liquor?
Every other store in the hood
So just pick one
Eenie, Meanie, Minie, Moe
There go another victim
Convict him
Lawyer fees

Eviction
Bankrupt his family
Take them all with him
It's sickening

Handed life sentence
From a county
That's illiterate
Institutional ignorance

Infections under scabs
I'm appealing it
Exposing the wound
Only way to heal the shit

Got my bloodline
Going alkaline
That's the bottom line
Marginalized

From the picket line
To the pipeline

They sold us pipe dreams
Daddy on that pipe
Still a Black king

Sumn in the water
Hard to stay clean

Sumn in the water
Poison babies

Got rashes on cheeks
But I'm irrational
If I choose to speak

Black and white
Ain't news to me
Feel more like
Noose to me
Desensitize
Can't feel my
Hands and feet
Paraplegic

To the country

I pledge allegiance
I'm constantly grieving

Instead of seeing it
Through my eyes
Incite violence from me

Well it's eye for an eye
So good thing
I got three

Part Two

My mother takes on a girlish disposition when she tells the story of how she met my father. Not as if she still has feelings for him, but as if she is still amused by his unique mannerisms and eccentricities. He is and was undeniably charming.

My dad was introduced to crack cocaine in high school by a friend whose father sold it. My father, much like my mother, was a victim of a certain kind of neglect that left him questioning his own worth and made him susceptible to being swallowed up. If his existence could go unacknowledged by his father, who shared his name, who lived in his city, for whom it would have required very little effort to pay him a visit, who created an entirely new family across town without regard for the family he left behind, then how would the world regard him? His mother, my grandmother Nancy, who attended college and worked a full-time job as a single parent of two by the age of sixteen, had little to offer in terms of experience or emotional support. Food on tables and clothes on backs epitomized parenthood and so long as basic needs were met, emotional needs could wait. He started by smoking cocaine and marijuana, but soon it became less marijuana and more cocaine.

At that time, the drug did not bear the same reputation it has now of ripping families apart and turning inner cities into battlefields. In fact, it held a certain prestige, romanticized by films like *Scarface* in the early '80s. It was not until violence peaked in America in 1991 that crack became a focus of media headlines, whose carefully constructed narratives worked to inextricably link the drug to the Black community. This gave way to the 1994 Crime Bill, which funded one hundred thousand new police officers and provided twelve billion dollars in federal subsidies for the expansion of state prisons, although crime was already decreasing by the time the laws were enacted. As throughout all American history, white people feared Black people and Black people feared for their lives. Every household in America was tuned in to *COPS,* which, as of 2022, has spent thirty-four seasons on the air. We were spoon-fed our daily dose of crack babies, junkie mothers, and absent fathers, and the systemic brainwashing infected us all.

This was the backdrop of my childhood. The perpetual fear and paranoia of a society indoctrinated with the same rhetoric that led to the legalized re-enslavement of Black Americans during Reconstruction. Like the 1994 Crime Bill, the Black code laws, which were enacted in 1865, facilitated a mass wave of imprisonment and forced labor across the South. It goes without saying that the essential structures and ideals upon which our nation was founded have not changed; they have simply grown more insidious and covert in nature. What happened in the '90s, and continues to play out today, was a war on Black people and poor people under the guise of a war on drugs. Because my parents dwelled at the intersection of both poverty and addiction, it was a war on them, and a war on me. My parents' terror, a culmination of all the terrorized Black people who came before them, became my own. And, like them, I carried the sum of that terror in my DNA.

I felt my father's fear every time those blue and red lights appeared in our rearview mirror. He was stopped once while speeding to pick

up my brother from a caretaker. I was in the back seat, still damp
and smelling of chlorine from having just finished swim practice.
But I had taken too long to change and now it was my fault that my
brother would not be picked up on time. I grew nauseous as soon as
I saw the lights and could feel myself beginning to panic—a child far
too familiar with holding space for the adults in her life by acting as a
scapegoat for their terror, which was often distorted into rage because
it could not be expressed authentically. My dad could not convey to
the officer how afraid he was of being arrested because it would mean
that his kids would be taken from him, or of being killed because it
would mean that we might be forced into the foster care system, or
simply of being late to pick up my brother because he did not have
the money to pay any late fees. He could not express his resentment
and discontent with the outside world, so he expressed it in the home.
Lacking autonomy in his interactions with the world perpetuated
his need for control and dominance in the only place where he held
authority. I knew I'd be blamed, and I accepted it. Children are often
victims of their parents' misguided anger—even the "golden child"
becomes the scapegoat sometimes. So that was my last swim class.

I felt my father's fear every time he'd go to check the mailbox,
knowing that he did not have the money to pay whatever bills he'd
been sent. Some days he'd just drive right past the mailbox that sat
at the end of the block, straight into the cul-de-sac where we lived,
avoiding the confrontation altogether. Even as an adult who has
escaped poverty, it requires courage for me to check my mailbox
and open my bills without anxiety, because I took on so much of his
stress. Piles of unopened envelopes took up residence on our kitchen

counter; there were even pieces of mail that remained unopened up until the point when we lost our house. In hindsight, I don't know why my father did not put the mail somewhere less visible. Its ever-presence was a sort of self-inflicted torture. A cruel reminder of his inability to sustain, which I imagine daily chipped away at his pride.

I felt my father's fear in the lack of affection he showed me. As a single father, he was terribly conscious of the possibility that one day I might grow up and misunderstand this affection as abuse or that it may be misinterpreted by outsiders. I did not speak much during those early years, causing several adults to make inquiries into this very matter. I then suffered the consequences of his humiliation. The truth was, I simply had nothing to say. Life had taught me that, in most cases, words were either completely empty or filled with lies. Moreover, this language that was passed down to me was insufficient and incapable of penetrating ears deafened by their owner's inner voices. I could not throw them around casually, as others seemed to do so well. My tongue was paralyzed by truth.

Months before my fifth birthday, my father and I relocated from my birthplace of Seattle, Washington, to Portland, Oregon. Portland was only a three-hour drive south of Seattle, so it was still close enough to visit but far enough to put space between him and his demons. There, he enrolled himself in a recovery program after splitting with my mother. My mother, consumed by her own addictions to drugs, alcohol, and men, remained in Seattle with my sister and continued to use. The day my dad announced to me that I would be going to live with him was the day one of my earliest survival mechanisms was formed. During his time in recovery, my dad made the drive back and forth from Portland to Seattle, often twice in the same day, to pick me up so that we could spend time together. He'd take me shopping, take me to get my hair done, take me to see family, and take me back home. Except this time, he did not take me back, and I, barely out of diapers and so closely bonded to my mother and sister, was afraid of the man with the booming voice who took so much pride in telling me that this would be my new home. I was convinced that my mother did not want me anymore—that I had done something wrong and was being punished for it. And because my sister and I did not share the same father and my dad was newly out of recovery and unable to extend his care beyond his own flesh, we were separated. I sat on the only piece of furniture in that hollow space, a bean bag in what would become our living room, and wept silently, shielding my small face with the palms of my even smaller hands in an attempt to spare my father's feelings.

Even at my young age, I had enough emotional intelligence to protect my father's feelings and enough self-awareness to know that mine were inconvenient. Lying and covering and stuffing was better than admitting my disruptive truth. And when my dad discovered me sitting there with my face shielded by my hands and asked me what was wrong, I lied and told him I was just excited. My dad did everything right, how dare I be so ungrateful? How could I sob in front of the man who vowed to father his children in a way he never was? So I grieved my mother's absence in silence. And I grieved her after every summer and every holiday that we spent together when I would return to my father's home. And the one time my father caught me grieving and I was bold enough to name the source of my pain, I was punished because she "didn't do shit for me." After that I no longer hid my tears; I simply stopped crying altogether.

Part Three

Maryanne was white with round hips, round lips, and reddish-brown hair broken up by streaks of blonde highlights, cut into a jaw-length bob. My father introduced me to his then-girlfriend and her biracial daughter, just one year younger than me, shortly after the move to Portland. They were already dating. I wonder now why he chose Maryanne. I wonder if subconsciously he associated his previous perceived failures, first with his mother and then mine, with Black women. I wonder if he saw her whiteness as a clean slate, a blank canvas, a fresh start—a space where he would be absolved of all previous shame and guilt for not living up to the expectation of what a Black man in America is told he should be. A space where no one could hold him accountable for not filling that role, however unfair and toxic that role may be. Or perhaps he associated whiteness with success—like many of the Black men who came before him and after him—and Blackness with all of the unfairness in his life. Perhaps he thought it best to put space between him and his past by putting space between him and his Blackness. He graduated from his recovery program and was hired at The Gap—grateful they took a chance on him despite his being newly sober—and secured a managerial position after working his way up from the sales floor. Perhaps Maryanne was symbolic of his having made it. A small consolation prize for his successful assimilation. I know for certain part of him desired that I have a mother figure, and with my mother far away and strung out, perhaps he thought this was the next best thing. Despite whatever unspecified factors brought them together, within three years they were married, divorced, and parents to a newborn baby boy named Kenny.

Although she came from an upper-middle-class white family, who played a significant role in caring for her daughter and me while my dad worked around the clock, Maryanne had her own vices, which were only made worse by the pressures of marriage. The divorce was filed after her daughter and I came home from school one day to discover that our piggy banks had been emptied and that Maryanne's gambling addiction was the cause. I do not know the source of Maryanne's discontent, but it only escalated from there, and by the time Kenny was seven years old, she was serving time in federal prison for fraud.

* * *

Tina was brown-skinned with a petite frame and loosely coiled hair that I admired for its beauty and envied for its ability to be molded and styled with ease. The hair salon where she worked was sandwiched between the market and a laundromat that sat on a piece of property owned by Big Daddy. My dad took the five-dollar-an-hour job at 18th and Dekum Street Market after he and Maryanne divorced and he, without the help of her parents, was left with no one to care for me. Every day after school I joined my dad at the market, where I would complete my homework before handling tasks around the store. Like every other corner store in the hood, we sold hot links, hot pickles, LaffyTaffy, licorice, Icehouse beer, ice-cold soda, chips, chicken, shrimp, Swishers, cigarettes, cigarillos, and other household necessities. I was nine years old at the time and worked the register while my dad worked the kitchen. When my dad and Tina started dating, he got a job at Comcast as a sales representative, and instead of working the register after school, I sat at the salon and watched her do hair. I absorbed the salon gossip, devoured every *Jet*, *Ebony*, and *Essence* magazine I could get my hands on, and inhaled the smoke emitted from pressing combs being run through freshly relaxed hair, including my own.

As an adult I learned that there was a fight between Tina's mother and my father that led to their breakup, but in that moment, I was once again the scapegoat. My father said if I was able to talk, instead of sitting in silence as I had often done, then maybe she would have been happier. After having three boys, my brother Sa'Von and two sons from a previous relationship, she was fixated on the idea of raising a daughter, but I was not like most girls my age. I did not like frilly socks and tank tops with lace around the collar that made my chest itch. I preferred backpacks over purses, and I lost the earrings she bought me because I took them out at school, stuffed them in my desk, and forgot about them. I needed a caretaker, she needed a project, and neither of us could be what the other needed.

The first time I understood addiction not as a disease in and of itself but as a symptom of mental and emotional distress was in the months following their breakup. Tina's salon changed locations, my father lost his job at Comcast after a white woman wrongfully accused him of sexual misconduct in an attempt to procure his position, and he ended up back at the corner store market. Three children, no wife, no girlfriend, no "real job." Every night he'd come home with a can of beer, go into his room, and close the door. The bills piled up just as quickly as the beer cans, and eventually the lights and water began being temporarily shut off and I, at twelve years old, was forced to take on the responsibilities of a wife and mother. The tasks of getting my brothers up for school, riding the bus with them across town, dropping them off, making sure they were fed, and cleaning the house by the time my dad returned home from work were all now my responsibility.

On Sundays, I'd get my brothers ready for church and wait for Sister Nicole to pick us up while my dad stayed behind, locked in his room with his beer for fear that the church's condemnation and hypocrisy would invite even more judgment into his life—judgment he simply did not need. I loved God, I loved Jesus, I loved church, I loved the songs, I loved the dances, I loved the pastor and his rhythmic soliloquies, I loved the first lady and her perfectly bumped ends, I loved the mothers of the church who dressed in all white and wore extravagant hats, I loved the ushers and their unceasing politeness, I loved the stained-glass windows, I loved the cornbread and black-eyed peas they served in the basement after the preacher finished preaching. I attended service on Sundays and youth group on Wednesdays, volunteered to pass out food for the homeless on Saturdays, and I wasn't going to be stopped because my dad no longer wanted to attend. I needed to have faith that one day my life would be better, even if it wasn't until after I was gone from this physical plane. I was a sponge, absorbing every syllable that bounced off the pastor's lips and observing every bead of sweat that poured from his forehead as he proclaimed the mighty word of God. Those experiences built the foundation of my faith, from which I have never deviated too far, regardless of the church's imperfections.

Part Four

Growing up in poverty does not equate to wanting less—our desires do not go away because we cannot meet them—it simply means we minimize our wants because we understand they aren't as urgent as electricity and running water. This shrinking of one's desires is not limited to the physical. In fact, it first takes place in the psyche, in the making small of a child's emotional needs—a theft that dictates how they will interact with the world for the rest of their lives, particularly as it pertains to romance and relationships. As a child I grew afraid of asking for things. I was afraid to ask for the required school supplies. I was afraid to ask for new shoes when my feet got too big for my old ones. I was even afraid to ask for help when I needed it. I became a child without needs who grew into an adult without needs and subsequently found myself in relationships where my needs weren't being met or were ignored altogether. But how could my needs possibly be met if I had never validated them or learned to express them in the first place? How could I expect someone else to do for me what I had never done for myself? Truthfully, by the time I was an adult, I did not even know what my needs were, only that they should come last, and the experiences I attracted were a projection of this subconscious belief.

* * *

My father, burdened by the pressure to provide, did not have the emotional capacity to coddle me nor did he have the financial capacity to indulge me, so it was my duty to protect his pride by making myself small and keeping him unaware of the things I needed. This kept me similarly unaware and eventually incapable of communicating my needs to future partners. His ego depended on my obliviousness to his financial hardship, and I was painfully aware of this fact. A sort of forced awareness that was acquired through consequence, because when you are poor, there are major consequences for minor mistakes. I once left the milk out on the kitchen counter while rushing to get ready for school and found myself sitting up in my room as punishment for the next two weeks. I am certain it was not the carelessness that I was being punished for, as my father claimed, at least not entirely, but the stress it would cause for him to find a few more dollars for another gallon.

The summer following my seventh-grade year, my father and I lost our home. We were rear-ended earlier that year; I remember the smell of the white powder that filled the air when the airbags exploded and not much else. My finger was broken, he was taken to the hospital with neck and back injuries, and our car was totaled. His physical pain only compounded and intensified the emotional pain that already consumed him. When the Vicodin the doctors gave him to manage that pain ran out, he returned to his old thing. My father made the down payment on our home using money he earned from The Gap's employee stock purchase program, which deducted a percentage of his paycheck each month and put it toward company shares. When he found the house, he cashed out on his shares and quickly made the purchase. It was not just the home, but the possibility of getting custody and having a safe place to raise me that excited him the most. It was the greatest accomplishment of his life. Proof to others of his adequacy as a parent and proof to himself that he was more than a former drug addict. He had done what all

Americans are told they should do, and this was monumental. Except that summer, America, on the brink of a recession, refused to make good on her promise, leaving us and thousands of other families— mostly poor and minority—to suffer the repercussions. He called the bank several times on that final day to let them know he'd come up with the money, but they wanted to take that house from us and would not let him pay.

My father shouted up the stairs one afternoon for me to come down so that we could talk. His tone was cool, but the day was warm and the sun was shining in through the living room windows. When I got downstairs, he was seated on our deep burgundy sofa. I sat next to him and, before he could utter a word, he began to sob. This terrified me. For the first time in my life, I saw my steel-willed dad— whose righteous indignation often kept him from the very things he desired—show what society has convinced men is a sign of weakness. But in the context of our living room, this was a moment of great strength. For that brief instant the mask fell off, and I bore witness to his heart as he poured out to me his feelings of failure. A moment of authenticity untainted by the expectations that haunted him. He had already failed, so what was the use in pretending any longer. Under all that fear and rage was a man with something to prove. A boy who questioned daily his father's love for him. A lover whose addiction he gifted to the woman of his dreams. A son whose mother gave him the twenty dollars he used to catch the Greyhound from Seattle to Portland to get clean and start a new life. A single parent with three children, and three baby mothers. An employee who worked at his grandfather's market for less than minimum wage. An individual who needed to demonstrate for his friends and family that he had truly turned his life around. A recovering addict ashamed of the recycled habits he could not seem to shake. Above all else, a father afraid of letting his daughter down. For the first time in my life, I felt as though I finally saw him as himself. Not as my parent, but as a human being. As Stober Davis.

Part Five

I began attending DaVinci Middle School in the sixth grade, which is also when I began to speak. As it turns out I was fluent in many languages. Languages not of the tongue, but of the heart and soul, such as dance and film and theater. DaVinci was a public school that offered a creative curriculum rather than the standard curriculum decided upon by the state. Art wasn't just an elective but an integral part of the entire school's structure. Despite being one of only a handful of Black students, which never made me feel exceptional but rather made me feel alone, I grew to love it. We danced jazz instead of P.E. We read and wrote poetry. We learned geography by studying world mythology. The arts-centric curriculum finally gave me the tools I needed to share my innermost truths and slowly peel back the layers of apprehension that had grown thick around my psyche. My feelings and thoughts were made valid through my creations, which further fueled my fire. Art was the permission I needed to simply exist. A reason for my being. A conduit that gave meaning and order to the chaos of my life and allowed me to transmute it into something beautiful. Even (but especially) my father noticed this change. I felt as though I could finally express myself to him in a dialect that required no words but that we both understood. And despite his lack of emotional and financial resources, he was involved. He never wanted me to question his love for me as he had questioned his father's. So he was present for parent-teacher conferences, chaperoned field trips, and attended dance recitals, but none of this familiarity with the school would prepare him for the choice he would have to make two years later. He would either have to take me with him back to Seattle, where he planned to start over once more after losing our home, or leave me in Portland under the care of my literary arts teacher, Ms. Wasson, who I had grown close to and who benevolently opened her home to me after learning of our situation. He, having witnessed a blossoming in me that he had never witnessed before, chose the latter. My dad moved to the city of Federal Way, just thirty minutes south of Seattle, and I spent the remainder of that summer after seventh grade with my mother and sister just like I always had, except this time, when I returned to Portland in late August, our home was no more.

That year with Ms. Wasson changed me irreversibly. As a healed adult I now recognize the divinity in this series of seemingly unfortunate events, which lead to my forced proximity with someone who could help foster my literary prowess. I performed a solo in the school dance recital. I landed a speaking part in the school play. I placed second in the eighth-grade poetry slam. I delivered the eighth-grade commencement speech. I even started my period, which Ms. Wasson and her mother, Nona, whom she lived with, commemorated by taking me out to dinner. Nona found my soiled underwear stuffed down in my laundry hamper while washing clothes. Having been raised by a man, I was terrified and in denial of this unfolding of womanhood. But rather than making a fuss, she showed me where the pads were under the bathroom sink and taught me how to use them. When the school year ended and I moved back to Washington, the contrast between my two experiences became unbearably apparent and the fallout was cataclysmic. I was unable to shrink myself back into who my father expected me to be, the version of myself he needed me to be so that his world could go on uninterrupted. My tongue rejoiced, for it had finally tasted freedom, and the Ebonee he knew only a year prior was long gone.

As summer came to a close, just days before the beginning of the school year, my dad had not yet figured out a plan to care for my brother Kenny, whose mom was incarcerated. My father, still in the midst of relapse and lacking better judgment, was content with me missing the first few weeks of freshman year to look after Kenny and expected that I should be content, too. I'd spent the months prior confined to his small, hot apartment caring for both of my younger siblings while he worked, loading and unloading luggage at Sea-Tac airport. He was gone before we woke up each morning and retuned after we were asleep. My inner child had just been granted the permission and provided the safety she needed to come out and play, and I had to put her away, yet again, so that I could take on the roles of wife and mother. By the end of those three months, I could no longer keep up the act. My needs, both physical and psychological, had changed. I was a young woman now. I could not foresee myself stuffing down my desires or stuffing tissue into my underwear every month when I bled because of the guilt of knowing he could not afford pads.

One evening I wrote a letter to my father, which I left sitting on the kitchen counter for him to discover upon returning from work. The letter detailed my discontent and ended with a request to live with my mother for high school. The next day, without a word, he gathered my things—which were still packed in boxes from our home in Portland—loaded up his car, and drove me to my maternal grandmother's house. There, he told me to get out, dropped the boxes on the curb, and only parted his lips to say, "never speak to me again," before speeding off.

I did not cry. In fact, I hardly felt a thing. What use were feelings in a moment like that? If my own father could not hold my feelings, there was certainly no one who could now. And so I held them myself, just as I held the boxes full of possessions, and made my way up the stairs to Lala's front door.

For Daughters

This is for daughters of mothers who came and went, daughters
of codependency
For daughters of mothers who wished them happy birthday over
the phone
For daughters who raised siblings as if they were their own children
For daughters who cried silent tears and hugged pillows because they
missed their mothers
For daughters who only saw their mothers on holidays and summer
breaks
For daughters whose mothers weren't around to tell them they
were beautiful
For daughters who carried their mother's karma
For daughters who learned from their mother's mistakes instead of
her teaching
But this is also for daughters who honor their mothers, daughters
who call their mothers Queens
For daughters who never stopped putting their mothers on pedestals
For daughters who would give their mothers the world
For daughters who became alchemists, transforming darkness to light
For daughters who know there's a blessing in every lesson
For daughters who figured out that loving yourself is being proud of
where you come from
For daughters who found power in forgiveness
For daughters who came to view their mothers as daughters
For daughters who will become mothers and affirm the value of
their daughters
For daughters who bow their head and thank God for their mothers.

Mother
Part One

My mother never took showers. In my entire life, I only recall seeing her shower twice, and neither of those times were until I was in high school. Instead, every night around 6 p.m. she'd draw a bath and soak her aching muscles in preparation for another shift at The Sands. Two things I have come to understand about my mother, things that I wish I had understood sooner, because they have offered peace and shifts in perspective. One, she is and was a healer. Men came to her, lost in the trouble and trauma of their daily lives, and she gave them a way out of their pain. And two, my mother was a star. She captivated and dazzled, and, just like the stars in the night sky, her six-foot statuesque build demanded most look up to see her. It is the very same energy she cultivated on that stage at The Sands, the ability to emote through body language, that was passed down to me and afforded me my success on the world stage as a model and actress. She danced in the darkness so that I could dance in the light. My blueprint was hers first. My desires, my potentials, my yearnings, all lived inside of her, but she was forced to abandon them for a reality that did not permit otherwise. The family and time period she was born into, the friends she made and the men she met along the way, and having two children to provide for by the age of twenty-one, made her dreams too far out of reach. The very same intuitive gifts I have so heavily relied upon in this lifetime dwelled inside of my mother first—misunderstood, punished, and not able to be fully actualized.

Perhaps drugs as a means of escape, for both my mother and the Black community at large, is not some moral failure on the part of each individual, but an attempt to make contact with a divinity that we were systematically made to feel does not reside within us.

Perhaps this is the reason why so many of my ancestors have often found themselves caught in the jaws of drugs and alcohol. From limitless creators to expressionless drones, generations of suppression meant generations of separation from our divinity. I am deeply saddened by the thought of souls incarnating on earth and being traumatized into submission, unable to self-actualize and bring to fruition all that is alive within. In the early 2000s, my mother began her own clothing business, selling urban brands like Apple Bottom, Evisu, and Baby Phat before they'd ever reached mainstream popularity. When it was time for me to return to Portland toward the end of each summer, she'd send me home with a suitcase full of brand-new clothes. Unfortunately, after just a few years as an entrepreneur, she was forced to close up shop and return to working full time at the club. But despite how few the years were, her time as a business owner was a highlight of her life, evidence that her dreams could never be completely tarnished.

To align myself with my potential and awaken to my deepest calling has been excruciating work and I have cultivated a great deal of empathy for my mother as a result. Admittedly it has taken quite some time for me to adopt this new perspective. It wasn't until I auditioned for the role of an exotic dancer and had to personify the same energy I saw her exude that I understood how the divine intelligence that governs our universe handcrafted each of my life's circumstances to make me more whole by allowing me to understand the energetic patterning I am comprised of. What I perceived as shortcomings were not shortcomings at all, but gifts wrapped in unexpected packaging. To see my blueprint not as a curse but as a gift that only I possess, an energy that only I can embody, a frequency that is unique to me, a vibration that cannot be replicated, is the ultimate self-love and, therefore, the ultimate freedom. I once thought that forgiveness was the apex of healing, and it is certainly powerful, but through experience I have come to discover that true healing occurs when a person realizes there is nothing to forgive, only acceptance to offer and shame to be released.

I have seen first-hand how the shame we carry, especially as Black people in America who have been made to feel ashamed about every aspect of ourselves, perpetuates the cycle of oppression we experience and keeps us out of our power. Just imagine what it would be like if we collectively decided that what has happened to us has been *for* us instead? What if we shared the things we have been taught to keep secret? What if instead of resenting those assigned to raise us, we sought to understand their behavior so that we could better understand what seeks to bind us? What if we simply accepted ourselves? Imagine how many cycles of behavior would be broken with this radical reframing of our childhoods and early lives.

* * *

After washing her body, my mother would stand up, tapping the top of each foot on the side of the tub as she stepped out, which made a thumping noise as excess water splashed back into the bath. She'd then grab a towel and dry herself off the exact same way, in the exact same order she did every day. Next was her makeup. I'd sit on the toilet, watching her at the sink, fixated on her movement as she transformed from Michelle to Misha Bell. When it came time to apply eye shadow, she would suck her makeup brush to wet it so that the teal color would adhere to the fibers and pop vibrantly against her olive skin. My sister did not care for these things, so this time was just between my mother and me. She worked nights, which made her nocturnal for the most part, so the time we spent together in the bathroom was sacred.

My mother returned from the club a little after 2 a.m. each day. Sometimes her then-boyfriend would pick her up after work, but most times she took a taxi home. For that reason, all the yellow taxi drivers in the North End knew her by name. A DUI in her early twenties prevented my mother from ever obtaining a license, so she did not drive, legally at least. She still drove to the store to buy groceries for dinner and new thigh highs for work, but generally we took the bus while her boyfriend drove her car. I say *her* car because, although he was the primary driver of it, the money came out of her pocket, gas money included. It both sickened and saddened me to watch my mother be taken from in this way. And by a man who treated her with not even a basic level of kindness or respect. Like a parasite that feeds on its host while simultaneously destroying it. For my mother, my sister, and me, getting out of the house each day was an act of liberation, and our enjoyment was an act of rebellion. An opportunity to exhale after holding our breath. An opportunity for her inner child to run free just as ours did.

Our daily routine consisted of waking up in the morning around ten or eleven, getting dressed and checking the bus schedule so that we could catch one downtown for lunch. Dim sum, teriyaki, sushi, Indian, Ethiopian, gyros, pho, my mother made sure I was no stranger to international cuisine. This she inherited from her mother, Lala, who took the entire family to a Chinese buffet every Christmas instead of cooking a traditional meal. Food was her love language, and so it became my mother's. Only my mother, and perhaps my sister, would understand the significance of my now being able to order duck noodle soup to my door through a delivery app. To this day, when I introduce her to new friends or tell her about someone new I'm dating, her first question is not about what kind of work they do or where they are from, but always, "Do they eat like us?"

My mother was a messy eater and so was my sister. I wasn't, because my dad would not let me be. There was rarely a time my mother left a restaurant without a stain on her shirt, which was fine with her because she rarely dressed up in anything fancy during the day anyway—a baggy white tee, grey sweatpants, and a pair of white K-Swiss. I suppose she saved all the glamour for the stage. At home she was goofy and childlike, sometimes to a fault. A vast departure from the seductress she became after nightfall. She dished out wet willies and passed gas loudly in public, always blaming it on one of the kids. She grew older in years but never in mind or heart. I realized when I went to live with her as a teenager that, although I am her daughter, my soul was chosen to parent hers. Perhaps this is how nature works; each generation, equipped by natural selection with a greater intelligence than the generation before, becomes the parent. Not in years, but in frequency and vibration. After lunch we would return home so that my mother could rest before waking up that evening and doing it all over again.

Dance in the Light

I am in every way a reflection of you
A replica of your love

You are my origin
Your womb is my native land
Your crass vernacular my native tongue

I am indigenous to all the parts of you
Colonized by those who should not have had the privilege
Of knowing the smooth of your skin nor the texture of your touch

You have given me life beyond measure,
What you have passed down to me cannot be quantified
By this system and its need to compare . . . its quest for more

I am the recipient of an invisible inheritance
There will be no martyrdom, only celebration
There will be no sacrifice, only unconditional giving according to
    my own free will
There will be no taking, only offering

It is because of you that I know the difference
Because I watched you dance in the shadows
Lacking grace at times but never stopping,
Never still,
Never slowing down

And so now I dance in the light

Part Two

My mom was selfish in all the ways a parent can be, yet honest in all the ways most parents are not. Thus, I simultaneously loved her and resented her deeply. Her vulnerability, her transparency, her inability to mask her demons, if only long enough to ensure that my sister and I would have something to eat before escaping back into her own reality, removed any level of expectation that a child might have for their caretaker. "Newport Kings in a box," the cadence of her voice as she ordered her favorite pack of smokes still lingers in my memory. She never attempted to uphold any conventional method of raising children or subscribe to any ideal image of motherhood. Her demons danced in the daylight and, because the survival of our family depended on her ability to seduce strange men, she could not afford the luxury of shame.

My mother's addiction began when she was seventeen years old, but, as any addict knows, addictions are not formed at the time you come into contact with the substance. They exist deep within the psyche long before that moment; I know this because I, too, was born an addict—searching for a way out. Addicted to the possibility of a life without pain. Perhaps it was growing up biracial in the '70s—a time of great social unrest with only her biracial brother to validate her existence and nobody to affirm the beauty of her thick, coarse hair. Or perhaps it was the neglect she felt as the child of an absent father, and with a mother who prioritized her own happiness over that of her children; a mother who did not take action to defend her daughter against the abusers and boogeymen; a mother whose need for love overshadowed the needs of her children, which made her susceptible to being swallowed up. Whatever the case, she did not accrue these curses on her own, they were heirlooms passed down in her lineage, and so she became equal parts terrorized and terrorizer.

When my dad recalls the story of how he met my mother, I still hear the love on his lips. It is a soft spot to land among the rubble. My heart beats faster to catch up with his. The admiration in his tone for the six-foot, fair-skinned, hazel-eyed "goddess" is palpable. My parents loved each other. He had no intention of harming her or going from the object of her affection to the instigator of her torment. He introduced her to crack cocaine while they were both employees at a fast-food restaurant on the Seattle waterfront. First it was a party thing for him, then it was an everyday thing, and by the late '80s they were doing it together. My sister came first, a year and eleven months before me. By the fall of 1992, I had arrived. My sister was conceived at a time when my parents were temporarily separated, so we do not share a biological father, but this information was withheld from my dad until months after she was born. My mother was twenty-one. I can imagine her fear and guilt, buried deep beneath layers of emotional debris, only masked by her dependency. My father was twenty-six. I can imagine his pain and the sting of betrayal. Or perhaps, even, a small moment of internal retribution—a covering for his own guilt. After all, he owed her one. Whatever his feelings for my mom, he loved my sister. He named her, he raised her, and he continued raising her even after learning she was not his.

I only know what my parents have told me about those first few years. My father tells me about the Christmas of '94 and how he worked overtime to afford gifts and stayed up all night to make the drive from Portland to Seattle in Big Daddy's candy-red 1964 Lincoln. He arrived at my mother's house first thing in the morning, eager to make sure his girls knew they were loved. I don't remember, but he'll never forget. He also tells me about the motel from which he cared for us while my mother took up work at a local club. My mother's physique is not what one might imagine when they think of an exotic dancer. She was slim in her teens and early twenties, but after having two kids there was no place on her body that stood firm besides her exceptionally strong calves. She was busty and her thick thighs rubbed and jiggled and stuck together when she walked around unclothed, which was quite often. But her thighs needed girth. Her thighs fed my sister and me. Her thighs fed the landlords and the bill collectors and the drug dealers. Her thighs bought groceries. Her thighs ran for buses and caught yellow cabs back and forth to the club every night. Her thighs paid for track and cheerleading and a back-to-school wardrobe every September. Her thighs were life-sustaining, and yet I despised them. When I hit puberty, I feared that one day my thighs might rub and jiggle and stick. It was not the weight, but the becoming like my mother that frightened me. Each new stretch mark of mine represented the possibility that one day I might become anything like her—my mother, who did not value her body, who was willing to commodify her own flesh.

Today's media has made normal what, in my childhood, filled me with great embarrassment. I rejected my femininity and my feminine body because I watched the way my mother used hers. I watched her work until her feet were sore and still allow a man to control her and dictate how she spent her money. I watched her pack up her home and move to Las Vegas as she chased that man across state lines, and he chased after another woman. To that man that took a metal hanger to her back, I watched her give away the love I believe she owed me and my sister. Her actions repulsed me, even as a child. I did not empathize with her then as I do now, I only saw weakness in her. Every year my mother's address changed to wherever he wanted to go. My sister was constantly uprooted and forced to adapt. It is not an exaggeration to say that I both loved my mother and hated her deeply for subjecting all of us to this torment, but herself especially.

Part Three

My Uncle Michael committed suicide in 1997, just a few days before Christmas. He played professional baseball for the Houston Astros, but after a dispute with the head coach that led to being cut from the team, he was catapulted into the trenches of depression and addiction. On that December afternoon, my grandmother received a phone call from my cousin Patrick that she needed to come home right away; my Uncle Michael was dead. Upon arriving at the scene, she discovered that he had hung himself in her stairwell. To this day she maintains that it was a group of thugs Michael was indebted to who killed him and that he would never do such a thing. Just as the coroner prepared to remove his body, she saw him there stretched out on the gurney and, in that moment, time froze. Her world stopped spinning. Her baby boy, the only of four children, was gone.

As I ascended my grandmother's staircase in the summer of 2007, after being left there by my father days before my freshman year of high school was to begin, belongings in tow, I cautiously pushed past the tools, wires, pieces of lumber, old newspapers, clothes, and electronics that crowded her doorway. Junk accumulated in every corner of her home except for the narrow path that led from the front door to the kitchen and up to the space where we all slept: my grandma, her boyfriend, myself, and my sister, who had recently been diagnosed with bipolar disorder and stayed up all night browsing the internet, which prevented any of us from getting adequate rest. Her house became a time capsule, a shrine to my uncle, and she threw nothing away. I tried once to remove some junk from the area where I slept and was met with rage. There was a time as children when my sister, my cousins, and I would eat fruit out of my grandmother's garden, lay outside in the summer sun, and roll around underneath her cherry trees, but those days were long gone and what had once been a fertile oasis and escape from the cruelty of my mother's boyfriends became a burial ground—a place where things went to rot and be forgotten about. I spent the next four years in and out of that blue house on the busy street with its unlivable living room, rat piss–soaked basement, fruit fly–filled kitchen, and the ants that I'd find crawling in bed next to me as I slept.

I tried sleeping on my mother's sofa for a few months during freshman year, but after being left in the small apartment she shared with her then boyfriend, my sister, and my sister's boyfriend for several days at a time with no groceries and no way to get in contact with her, only to discover the methamphetamine pipe lodged under her mattress, I ended up back with my grandmother. Sophomore year, after my mom moved into the house my Uncle Michael bought before his death, which my grandmother took possession of and rented out, I tried living with her again, only to be met with bitter consequence. One evening while my mother was out getting gas on a busy Seattle street known for lascivious conduct, a man approached her and offered her an opportunity to make some money. Aging out of the strip club industry, newly single, and in need of work, she obliged, but soon found herself being stalked, beaten, and harassed. (She shared with me that, in retrospect, she feels this experience was her karma for all of the pain she inflicted on her children and everyone around her during her years as an addict.) After moving the man into our home, my mother began working as an escort, posting classified ads online, and engaging sexually with numerous strangers each day in the bed where I laid my head because the man did not want her engaging with them in their bed. Lubricant and condoms were a staple on my nightstand and a constant reminder of what went on while I was at school each day, where I was terribly afraid of my mother's secret being found out. The thought of walking down the hallways of my high school only to be confronted by cruel remarks from reaction-seeking upperclassmen like, "We saw your mom online last night," ate away at me. How would I react? I know the most honest part of me would demand that I burst into tears and release the pain instead of trapping it in my body, but at that time there was no space for tears. I would have to stuff it down and pretend to be unbothered or I might join in and laugh with them, all the while dying a slow death inside and housing an ever-expanding hatred of self.

The Letter

Recently, my mother asked me to write a letter for her.

I assumed that it would have something to do with legal or
      medical needs.

After all, my mother's middle school education makes her a less
      than proficient communicator by social standards.

She went on, however, to tell me that the recipient of the letter
      she wanted me to write would be her mother, my grandmother.

It needed to be said that she felt unloved. That my grandmother
      prioritized her work, her men, and her other children, and had
      nothing left for her youngest daughter.

But my mother also wanted it to be clear that she would continue
      loving anyway. And if by chance my grandmother wanted to
      reciprocate that love, she would be open to it.

A few years back my mother pinched a nerve, which resulted in her
      inability to move as she once did.

Since then, it's been in and out of the hospital, scare after scare.

With my mother almost twice my age and my grandmother three
      times, I'm not sure whose mortality she fears more and why
      she feels this sudden sense of urgency.

But what I do know is this:

I know what it's like to want nothing more than a parent's love
To simultaneously feel not good enough and too much
Parrot my parent's apparent perfection
Placed on pedestals, never calling out bluffs
Watching my mother use love as a crutch
Never unconditional, just something to hold her up

I know what it's like to want to be the one chosen
Instead, I was "first" in line . . . after men, money, cars, houses, and
     clothing

My mother told me I had a nose
That was of my father's molding
And more than ugly, it made me feel like the only
Unable to see myself reflected in the one who bore me

I've come to learn self-hate is a poison
And it was probably 'cause HER Canadian mother
Made her texture seem like torment

Biracial beedeebeedz down the back of my mother's neck
Made her a target for bullies and disrespect

She tells me how she was always lonely
No one in the home so she relied on her homies
That's when the drugs became a part of her story

Half-caste castaway
Unwanted by the only one she wanted support from
And I relate to that 'cause my sister use to tell me all the time
I was suppose to be an abortion

I was only four when
My father took custody and moved me to Portland

He got clean but the separation left cracks in my heart
Why my mother didn't want me? Why we gotta be apart?
Broken promises, empty seats, and try again tomorrows
Blame it on the distance but what's the difference if I'm your
    daughter?
And that feeling becomes addicting
Chasing after someone that only leverages their interest
You learn that your value is only what you can give them
Make their life easier
Want for nothing
Trespasses too easily forgiven

Attracting men who don't know how to treat women
My first boyfriend was a pimp
And I was his first victim

Never sold no pussy
But my life was collateral
My family history what made our energy compatible

My mother knew about it and
And it ate away at me like a cannibal
Why you ain't stop me from playing the same hand as you?

Her example is what made the behavior acceptable
She was stuck in the mud
And the love I attracted tracked in that same residue

She sold her body for supplies I needed, back to school
Except she let a man ration back the amount he choose
And I begged her for those tennis shoes
The thought of what it cost now hard to swallow like unseasoned
    food

These patterns get passed down until they are confronted
I used to judge it, but how can I place blame on you?
I learned my mother was mishandled and
My grandmother dismissed it
One generation later
It happened to my sister
I'm starting to learn that every villain
Was once was a victim
I hated my mom without ever knowing her story
Like how these men more important than your children

But now as an adult I know how easy it is to become entrenched in
'Cause every day only thing separating me is one bad decision

But this isn't a poem about trauma it's a poem about healing
And how sometimes we want accountability from those who can't
    give it

I've learned over the years the heart works like a mirror
The more my heart breaks for her the clearer I can see her
And I empathize because we share the same feelings

If she never had a mother
How could she be?

I'm sure my mother had dreams that consisted of more
Than using her feminine curves to turn men into fiends
She danced on stages with poles and left the world stage to me
Blueprint in my genes, entertainment in my veins
I guess God intervened
Took her darkness and transformed the frequency
The shadows and the shame that came from shackled feet
Accepting she was exactly what I needed
Is how I set myself free
Recently, my mother asked me to write a letter for her
But it turns out
I wrote it for me

Sister

Growing up, I despised yet felt fiercely protective of my sister. What mutated into anger began as shame, which had even deeper origins in my desire to shelter her from the world. Unlike myself, my sister did not hide my mother's occupation from her peers, nor did she hide her own sexual curiosity. The way she allowed herself to be taken advantage of by anyone who offered her the possibility of love or friendship nauseated me, for I knew all too well the source of her perceived weakness. My sister spent most of her childhood locked away in her room, an accessory to my mother's chaos. Sex was all around us as infants and small children, and when we discovered my mother's porn collection, my sister would watch the tapes over and over as if they were Disney movies. By twelve, there was no space left between the desires of my mother's boyfriend and my sister's young body, but his perversion began much earlier. The eyeing, the noticing, the unchecked remarks directed toward her underage anatomy. Like too many young women, her early development made her a target of sexual violence, and my mom, preoccupied with her own abuse, remained unaware. We both feared his rage, but my sister, who resembled my mom with her fair skin and green eyes, and no father present to protect her, got the worst of it, and I, with my darker features resembling those of his own children, did not face the same wrath. He tormented her, psychologically and physically, and because he damaged her body, she damaged mine— even as an adult I have the scars to prove it. But after those three months out of the year and the holidays I spent with my mother, I was able to retreat back into the normalcy of life with my father, while my sister had no escape.

Maybe it is self-centered to think, but perhaps my sister's birth was in some way an offering, and she, being the first to hold space in the womb, absorbed the sins of my mother, my mother's mother, and the women who preceded her, whom I did not meet before their time on Earth expired, so that I could evade much of the karma passed down in our lineage. But I carried my own kind of karma, and later came to realize that understanding my sister's pain would be the key to unearthing and healing it. By five years old, I was certain that I would not bear children, a fact to which all of the adults in my family can attest. But what trauma might a five-year-old have withstood that could create this type of awareness, this type of certainty? I made a subconscious agreement with myself early in this lifetime, or in a lifetime before, that I would rather end my bloodline than pass down the unmet pain that lived inside of me, particularly as it pertained to sex. While my sister gave herself away, I became determined to keep it all together. And while my sister got stuck in her body, mentally dissociating from the world, I got stuck in my mind, and my body went numb as a means of survival. My nervous system could take no more, and I became affected neither by pleasure nor pain. I unconsciously deemed my body worthless, and that sense of worthlessness trickled into every aspect of my life to follow.

I went on my first date at sixteen years old and, when I returned home that evening, my mother was sat in the living room, waiting for me, intoxicated beyond coherence. She asked for my phone, and I handed it to her. A few seconds later she was screaming into it at the boy who had just taken me to see *Transformers*, the first to ever show any interest. Utterly embarrassed, I snatched the phone back, hung up, and quickly texted him apologizing, which immediately set her off. Belligerent and enraged, she began delivering blows to my 115-pound body. I ran to the kitchen, and she followed me. Cornered and in a panic, I kicked her in the stomach, hoping to incapacitate her momentarily so that I could get away, but it didn't faze her. It was as though she hardly felt anything. I noticed the vague look in her eyes, and it was only then that I realized this was not a fight I could win. I was not fighting my mother, I was fighting all of the pain that lived inside of her. I did not want to hurt her, but just as badly I did not want to be hurt, and so I left.

I moved in with my paternal grandmother, Nana, halfway through my junior year of high school, and for the first few months, things seemed to be going all right. She lived in a beautiful house situated on a plot of land big enough for two in the Central District, Seattle's historically Black neighborhood just minutes outside of downtown. Her love for me was palpable. When my father and Maryanne married, she made sure that my father did not move Maryanne into the house while I was away visiting my mother for the summer to prevent me from feeling ambushed. And when my father and Maryanne divorced, she took me on a girls' trip, just her and I, to make sure I was emotionally sound during the aftermath. She always made sure I knew peace in the midst of mayhem. The members of her book club, ski club, and Buddhist organization all knew Nancy's granddaughter, and she, having had her children so young, was almost always mistaken for my mother. Although I'm sure she found this flattering at times, it only served to further intensify her fear that I would one day do the same. And so that afternoon, when my grandmother walked downstairs and saw me sitting on her sofa next to the boy I invited over for dinner, the boy to whom thirty minutes earlier she had served her beef stew, it triggered something in her that could not be undone. She entered the kitchen, refilled her bowl, and walked back up the stairs in silence, a silence more violent and more lethal than any amount of fire power.

The following morning as my grandmother drove me to school, she let me know we'd be taking a trip to the gynecologist to confirm that I was still a virgin. Those were the terms if I wanted to continue living in her house. I had never even kissed a boy, let alone had sex. In fact, I was deeply ashamed of my own sexuality. As a child, my mother's perversion and overexposure to adult content drove me into complete denial of my own sexual nature. As a teenager, I would walk around the block on my return from school, waiting for the unrecognizable vehicles parked in front of my mother's house to be gone, because it meant my mother was inside with a client. As a child, I would beg my mother to clothe herself so that I could have friends over, and she'd shout, "This is my house! I don't give a fuck!" As a toddler, my mother would interact with my body and my sister's body in ways that were not suitable for a parent. Acts of foolish immaturity rather than abuse, but mortifying nonetheless. And all those times in between were equally mortifying. Although I found it repulsive then, I did not understand until I matured how vastly inappropriate and destructive it was for an adult, no matter their relation, to violate the autonomy of a child in that way, but that is how my mother liked to play. Besides, how could I expect my mother, lacking autonomy over her own body, to afford me mine? My mother, who allowed herself to become someone's property, replicating patterns of ownership that were embedded in our collective psyche during slavery and still played out in her present reality. So, although my grandmother was doing what she thought was right, Nana's ultimatum felt like yet another attempt at destroying that sovereignty, an act of violence to which I could not oblige.

When I did lose my virginity, it was the summer before my senior year of high school. Like my period, this initiation into womanhood took place much later for me than it did for my peers. It was not a romantic experience, nor was it anticipated. It is one that I hardly wish to remember, which serves me well, because I hardly do. It was at a party thrown by a classmate as the school year was coming to a close. We started at the beach and eventually made our way to a house—at least, that is what I am able to piece together from the depths of my memory. What I do remember clearly is blueberry vodka, anger, and tears from another girl who had a crush on the boy I'd "hooked up" with. It was the first time I'd ever gotten drunk and the first time I'd ever blacked out. One minute I was celebrating and the next I was giving my body to some boy for whom I had no feelings other than the lust provoked by my intoxicated state. I felt sensation where I had previously denied myself access as a means of survival. But if you do not face your shadow, it will come for you, and mine did. I do not blame him, because he was as drunk and incoherent as I was, but facing him at school the following week felt impossible. After waking up the morning after, before leaving, I went to use the bathroom, wiped myself, looked at the blood on the toilet paper from having been penetrated for the first time, and thought,

"I guess that's it." And then I began walking, with an unfamiliar pressure between my legs, until I reached home, just ten minutes away. And I kept that secret, until now.

Intimacy

Intimacy is a measurement of my proximity to truth.

Intimacy is a measurement of the space between me and God.

Between who I am and who I was created to be.

Between the manifested and the unwitnessed.

Between flesh and spirit.

Intimacy merges the two into one, destroying the illusion of separation.

Destroying the idea that I was ever disconnected from Source.

Destroying the idea that I was ever disconnected from you.

Intimacy leaves no room for judgment.

Intimacy removes the veil we hide behind and the fear that created it to begin with.

Intimacy is allowing.

Intimacy is openness.

Intimacy is vulnerability.

Intimacy is nakedness.

Intimacy creates space for unfiltered expression; it is a gateway to true essence.

In solitude, intimacy is experiencing God through myself.

In company, intimacy is experiencing God through another.

Intimacy is contact.

Eye contact.

Body contact.

Mind contact.

Energy contact.

And above all, intimacy is contact with the soul.

Caterpillar

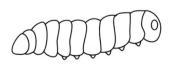

Survival

My heart breaks for
The version of myself
Stuck in survival

The version of myself
Who awaited my arrival

To a higher state of consciousness
Where there is no rival

No opposition
No idols
Where folks ain't too prideful
And my thoughts are unbridled

Soul been sucked out like lipo
Ain't "Type A," you a typo
Gotta stay in line tightrope
If not, you playing with pyro

No trampoline in this circus
No bouncing back
They just trample you

Speak too much truth
Lovecraft

They quick to cancel you

That type of thinking
Spread quick
Just like a cancer do
I'm starting to think
That the sickness
Was in the attitude

American dream
If you can
Throw a forward lateral or
Shoot a basketball
If not, they shoot you down
Just like an animal

Pimp you out
For profit
So the pain
Is understandable

Justified even
'Cause success
Wasn't the plan
For you

I feel for you
Haters salty

Brita for the bitter
Tryna filter you

Tryna fit your life
Inside a screen
That shit seem
Reel to you

Meanwhile you blocking all
Your blessings
Too much
Fear in you
My circle small
But we solid
Yeah, we spherical

Love myself a little
More each day
That's what
The healing do

Modeling

I bounced between my mother and her mother for the remainder of high school after leaving Nana's house. By graduation, I was the only Black student in my class to earn their International Baccalaureate diploma, which is not a testament to my exceptionality but a criticism of our nation's public schools, which systematically fail students of color. Ingraham High School was the only school left in the district that still had space when my mother took me to enroll. It was the kind of place you ended up if you'd been expelled for fighting or truancy—the kind of school where Black students were forced into standard-level classes while white students were encouraged to take advanced placement classes. For the most part, the newly excavated artist in me slowly receded back into the safety of my shadow as I learned to navigate this new space. The first semester of freshman year I was, however, able to take a theater class, and that's where I met Kiara. She was beautiful and chocolate with long hair that stretched down to the middle of her back. Soon she would be my best friend and I would be hers. We were both new in town and didn't have friends from middle school to help us acclimate to our new environment. She was from Greensboro, North Carolina, and I loved the way she talked; her southern vernacular was like music to my ears. She told me stories of Bojangles, which we didn't have in the Pacific Northwest, and I knew one day I needed to try a Bo-Berry Biscuit. She told me stories of the single intersection and the single stretch of dirt road that cut all the way through her town. She told me stories of the hot summer days and the dust that swilled about in the air from a lack of rain. Her father was a high-ranking military officer, and when her free-spirited mother, Drea, decided she'd lived enough of his rigid lifestyle, she packed up her children and moved to Seattle.

I saw a lot of myself in Drea, which was vastly different from my experience with my own mother. In fact, she was the first adult woman I saw myself becoming like in more than a success- or appearance-related way. My first real role model. Like Kiara, she was brown-skinned with beautiful, straight, very white teeth that were nearly too big for her mouth but somehow suited her perfectly. She was tall and lanky, much like myself and unlike Kiara, who inherited her father's shorter, more muscular stature. She was earthy and resourceful. Although she did not have a lot of money, she found ways to care for herself and create a sense of luxury. She would shop at Whole Foods and buy a jar of organic coconut oil, use nearly all of it, and then return it for cash just before it reached the bottom, stating that she was not satisfied with the product. Then she would take the cash and buy another. She was a strict vegetarian, and when Veggie Fest, Seattle's annual vegetarian food festival, would roll around, we'd roam the Seattle center stuffing ourselves with free samples. Drea was not a rich woman, but she was a smart one, who knew what she deserved. She never turned me away from her home or made me feel unwelcome. There was not much space, but it was always warm and always clean. The walls were covered with images of Black women that she had torn out of magazines and taped up. There was no man in the house except Kiara's little brother Patrick, who was in middle school. Everywhere I looked I saw myself honored, appreciated, valued, and cared for in a way that I had not before. I loved it there. Since neither of us drove, Kiara and I frequently caught the bus, an hour and a half from

Ingraham to her house and back. Just days after her little sister was born, she invited me over and we caught the number 41 across town so that I could meet her. We'd grown inseparable. We tried out for the cheer squad together. We auditioned for the school play together. We shared our deepest darkest secrets with one another. We were all each other had, but we were all we needed.

* * *

Kiara was initiated into motherhood and transferred schools before the start of senior year so that she could be closer to home—I am now the godmother to her son, Jay. A few months after Kiara left, I met Natalie. She did not attend Ingraham but played basketball, which meant frequent visits to other schools. Natalie's mom was like mine, so she was like me. As daughters of recovering addicts, much went unspoken but still understood. Whenever I needed an escape, she'd let me spend the night, hiding my thin frame under her comforter, disguised by her collection of throw pillows. As fate would have it, one bus line took me from right outside of Lala's North Seattle home directly to Natalie's home in West Seattle. God's plan unfolding without flaw.

A few months before the school year ended, I decided to act on my childhood dream and go for an open casting at a local modeling agency. By that point, after being moved around from home to home throughout high school, I needed, for my own sanity, to create something for myself—something that could not be taken away from me. I searched online and there were three agencies: Heffner, TCM, and Seattle Models Guild. I chose Seattle Models Guild. One

Tuesday afternoon, I cut class, because the casting was held from 1 to 2 p.m., and went in. There was one other girl in line ahead of me, so I waited, anxiously trying not to compare myself to her. She looked drastically different than me with her red hair and blue eyes, so this was nearly impossible not to do. I studied her nose and her waistline and how tall she looked when she stood up, for these were the things that, in my mind, separated me from my destiny. When they called my name, I hopped up and shuffled down the hallway, wearing the heels I had stuffed into my backpack. I was brought back into an office space where a kind man with brown hair, beaming brown eyes, and golden skin asked me some simple questions, took my measurements, and snapped a few photos. The next day he called to let me know that the agency was interested in signing me. To pay for my portfolio, I worked double shifts at the mall, making minimum wage until I had the $400 I needed for my first test shoot. My mom was there that day. She watched as I got my hair and makeup done for the first time, stepped in front of the camera, and delivered the best performance I knew how.

My first booking was e-commerce for Amazon.com and then for Nordstrom, which are both headquartered in Seattle. They'd book me once every couple of weeks and I'd have to cut class so that I could work. Some days they'd use my full body. Other days I'd spend eight hours on set having my photo taken from the waist down. Front and back, over and over, the pressure on my knees and back intensifying with every look change. It was not fun or glamorous, but it was a step toward my dream, and it paid $800 a day, which was more money than I'd ever had.

While driving on the freeway with my mom early in the summer of 2011, after having just graduated high school, an announcement came blaring through the radio that *America's Next Top Model* would be coming to Seattle, and they were hosting auditions. She begged me to audition, but I was reluctant. Although it was my dream from the time I was a little girl glued to the television screen, I was scared of what it might do to my relationship with Seattle Models Guild or that it might hurt my career. Back then, reality TV show contestants were not taken seriously within the fashion industry, and rightfully so. They were often framed as psychotic caricatures, dramatized for the sake of viewership and ratings. I wasn't prepared to give up the very small bit of success I had cultivated for the possibility of something greater. That's what being poor does to you. It keeps you afraid and locked in a pattern of survival so that when new choices present themselves, you remain crippled by fear. It becomes nearly impossible to trade consistency for possibility, even if that consistency makes you miserable or drains you of your lust for life. Besides that, I knew there would be hundreds of girls at the audition and thousands more across the nation vying for a spot on the show. But I obliged my mother and agreed to go. That fall, instead of taking introductory courses at the University of Washington as I had planned to, after a rigorous audition process, I joined the cast of *America's Next Top Model*: Cycle 18.

* * *

After two months in LA, traveling to Hong Kong, and celebrating my nineteenth birthday in a hotel room with a bottle of Absolut vodka and the remaining contestants, I placed fifth and returned to

Seattle to complete my freshman year of college. I loved attending the University of Washington, with its rusty red brick buildings and the rows of cherry blossom trees that lined the campus grounds and turned the walkways into wedding aisles when they'd bloom in spring. But after that semester, a lot of which was spent getting blackout drunk on Pinnacle Whipped Vodka and evading my home, I decided that living in Seattle was no longer part of my plan and that my time would be better spent moving to New York in pursuit of my modeling dream. In October 2012, at nineteen years old and with $700 in my pocket, I filled two suitcases and boarded a plane. My flight was one of the last to take off before air traffic was shut down due to an incoming storm. Hurricane Sandy hit full force the next day, knocking out all the power below 14th Street and flooding the Financial District. I found respite with Candice, another show contestant, and her mother. We sat in their Bed-Stuy brownstone and waited and listened to the sound of wind blowing, trees falling, and car alarms being set off. Although I was eager to move into my apartment and begin visiting agencies, I waited patiently for things to return to normal.

My eagerness soon proved to be futile. Now, I was not disillusioned by some romantic idea of the industry. I had done my research, and agencies never placed more than three or four Black girls on their board among a sea of blondes and brunettes. During that time it was also common practice for Black models to be shipped off to South Africa for months and forced to live in close quarters, where they'd accumulate debt in an attempt to build their portfolios within a primarily Black fashion market. Since the South African consumers were majority Black, Black models were more likely to be hired for commercial and editorial work. If they did well enough, agencies *might* be willing to take a chance on them upon returning to the United States. The odds were against me, but I was determined. I figured that once I landed a modeling contract, the industry would open up for me. But at every turn I was met with resistance. White agents with no knowledge of Black haircare would run their fingers though my weave and tell me things like, "We already have a girl with your look." Translation: All Black girls look the same. Or, "We don't think this is the right fit for you." Translation: We have reached our maximum capacity for Black models. But the most excruciatingly painful was, "We just don't know what to do with you." What I see now as an admission to their own incompetence felt like yet another attack, as if representing me would be some extraordinary challenge simply because of the color of my skin. When I did finally get signed, after being rejected over and over again, it was by an agency whose Miami office I'd signed with several months prior, during a scouting trip they took to Seattle. They were later shut down for their connection to and involvement in a human trafficking operation—degrees of which are hardly unique within the industry. Upon signing to the Miami office, a white male agent sat across from me and said my body was worth more than my beauty. My New York office welcome wasn't much different. It went something like this: "You probably won't ever make it to the cover of any magazines, but we might be able to make you a little cash. When one of our other Black girls isn't available, we'll push you."

Casting directors would ask, "Where are you from?" to which I would respond, Seattle. And then, "Where are your parents from?" to which I would respond, Seattle. I was met with looks of confusion, as if it were impossible to conceptualize that Black beauty exists in America. If they were really bold, they would ask, "But, like, what's your ethnicity, where are your people from?" to which, as a descendant of slaves, I could offer no adequate response. They'd say, "You're so beautiful, you must be mixed." What may have been intended as a compliment felt like an attempt to rationalize the source of my beauty. If I was mixed, it would all make sense. My proximity to whiteness would ease their curious minds. I was told that I should steer away from Black publications like *Essence* and *Ebony* magazines because if I got labeled an "urban model" fashion would close its doors to me. Although I am visually Black, to be labeled Black or to outwardly proclaim my Blackness meant to be stripped of value and pigeonholed into a world of subsidiary work. I could be Black, but only on the outside, and never in my speech or my thought or the way I moved through space.

I had my face painted grey by makeup artists who were reluctant to even touch my skin and I had my hair ripped from my head and burnt to the point where I had to chop it off and start over. Should I open my mouth in protest, I was immediately knocked back down into my place. "Another angry Black girl," they'd assume, to which there was no defense. There is no way to counter a stereotype so embedded in the collective American psyche that, rather than taking the time to listen, it's their first response whenever a Black girl has a differing opinion. When I didn't have the status in the industry that I have now, I was afraid of speaking up because I didn't want to get marked as difficult to work with. My livelihood was on the line, so I had to shut up and take it. I was told that I shouldn't complain because "at least I was doing well" and "there are a hundred other Black girls waiting to take my place." I was the "token Blackie" who made it, while the door remained closed for all others. I had to live within the confines of trite stereotypes that compressed me into a tiny box. I felt completely powerless. I was broken down mentally, physically, and emotionally. I felt like everything had been taken away—my identity, my autonomy, my ability to stand up for myself, any sense of who I was before I got into the industry—it had all evaporated.

Those stories of young girls taken advantage of and exploited by predatory photographers became my own. The sexualized persona I took on in my early years as a model was nothing more than a mask under which my inner child hid, desperately seeking sovereignty over her own body.

It is ironic that although I detested my mother's behavior, I fell into the same trap from which she could not escape because I had not yet made peace with the energy that ruled her. So that same energy took control over me. My sexual energy was up for grabs, because instead of acknowledging it, harnessing it, and using it for my benefit, as I learned to do further into my healing journey, I rejected it, thus rejecting my power and creative potential. I simulated sexy before I embodied it, because the repulsion I felt toward my mother polarized my psyche. At work, I was often asked to pose nude or in lingerie, while with partners I was prudish and found no pleasure in intimacy.

I had learned to dissociate from my body when exposed to the explicit, which, as a child, was often. I deemed myself broken, because my unexamined feelings kept me locked out of my body, and this was only confirmed by frustrated lovers who couldn't understand my lack of enthusiasm. Because of my internalized brokenness, I allowed my body to be fucked instead of made love to. I punished it for denying me the pleasure I believed I was owed, and I allowed others to punish it without apology.

* * *

Already ripped apart by the world, the Christmas following my first few months in New York, I returned home to one of the most devastating scenes of my life. I started dating my then-boyfriend when I was a senior in high school, and we remained in a long-distance relationship when I moved to New York. Our time as a couple was far from perfect; after all, each of us were only mirroring the love we'd known as children. My heartbeat accelerates at the thought of myself on the floor of my grandmother's living room, body pressed against her burnt orange carpet and appendages numb from lack of oxygen. I thought I was dying, and maybe I would have had my sister not walked into the room and seen me there, breathless, with tears rolling down my face. In a voice I did not recognize because my tongue had gone numb inside of my mouth, I cried out for her to call 911. Minutes later, I was in the back of an ambulance. Shortly after that, I was in a hospital bed being monitored. I was told I'd had a panic attack, the first I've ever experienced. Triggered by a series of phone calls unanswered, texts with no reply, an imagination that presumed the worst, and the wound of abandonment still festering. But he was my first love, and, like all first loves, I thought we would be together forever.

He was yellow with tattoos; full, round facial features; and gorgeous thick locks. I loved the way he dressed and the way his body moved when he walked. Such grace. He made music and I was enamored by his talent and ear for artistry—he introduced me to Kendrick Lamar, which was a big deal. I'd sleep on the floor with him in the studio he stayed at, because his mom lived in San Diego and he didn't have anywhere else to go and my living situation wasn't much better. A few months into dating, he received a message from a girl on Facebook saying that she wanted to make some money, code for prostitution, and that she hoped he could show her how. In love and not unfamiliar with that lifestyle, I agreed. This was normal in my world, so I accepted it. The night before I was scheduled to return to New York from Seattle, he had a show at a local venue, and I was in attendance along with all of our mutual friends. After his set, I went to the bathroom, where I ran into a well-known Seattle prostitute, who was surprised to see me there. She asked if I was still with him, to which I unwittingly responded, "yes." Then, with all the satisfaction in the world, she pulled out her phone to show me photos of the girl he was pimping. She was pregnant and it was his. I left the bathroom in disbelief, with my stomach twisted in knots and a golf ball in my throat. When I found him and confronted him about the pregnancy, he pushed me into the wall, shouted that it wasn't his, and told me to get out of his face. I returned home hysterical and heartbroken, but the worst of it had yet to be brought to light.

When my mom asked why I was crying, I told her what had just gone down, only to be met with utter indifference. That is when I found out that my mother and her boyfriend/pimp not only knew that he was sleeping with the woman he was pimping, but that they were all working together and worked out of the same house. My house. The house my grandmother leased to her. The house with my baby photos on the mantel. The house where I sat at the dining room table to do my homework in high school. The house where I allowed my boyfriend to stay when he was out of options. I boarded my flight devastated and horrified. What kind of mother does that to their child? What kind of boyfriend does that to their lover? I was in agony. I barely ate or slept for the next three weeks. A part of me broke that day that has taken nearly a decade to repair.

* * *

In retrospect, as I began the repairing process, it became clear to me that my experience with my first love locked me into a pattern of attaching my value to being of service, putting the needs of others before my own, and deferring my dreams so that I could be a catalyst for the aspirations of lovers and friends. Self-sacrifice under the guise of empathy; a perpetual victimhood that kept me trapped in cycles of exploitation and powerlessness. Although he did not initiate this subconscious energetic pattern, because its preexistence and my lack of awareness of it is what invited him into my space in the first place, he certainly exacerbated it. For this, I do not place blame.

Since America's conception, Black people have never been adequately compensated or compensated at all for our labor and, never having our value affirmed, it's been nearly impossible for us to recognize our worth and demand what we are owed. Capitalism, being slavery's successor, has made all Americans, not just Black people, victims to this way of thinking. As an entire human race, we have been trained to attach our value to what we do and the minuscule rewards that come from it, rather than who we are as individuals. This dynamic has manifested in our interpersonal relationships, which are simply microcosmic models of how we relate to the system. As Black people, everything in our upbringing enslaves us to unconsciousness—the films, the TV shows, the news, the magazines, the absorption of shame-inducing ideologies that do not belong to us.

And as Black women, we must cope with this perceived lack of value under the weight of misogyny and patriarchy with no awareness of who we are or what we are owed by virtue of our existence and with our value so often being reduced to our looks. Thus, this pattern of behavior, which has its origins in slavery and was further embedded within me during my childhood, took full control over my way of being once I began participating in romantic relationships.

Back in New York, low on money, self-esteem, or any true sense of value, I began dating again. This time with a guy about ten years older than me who had a reputation for hooking up with models and who partied and drank excessively—a lifestyle I quickly adopted. Every day I woke up ready to drink and every night I went out ready to dance. This lasted for about six months, until he told me he was no longer interested in me and that he didn't want a relationship, and things ended between us. It was difficult for me to let go, not because of the length or depth of our involvement but because I needed proof that there was existence after my first love, and that is what I projected onto him. He was a life raft, and I had just been cast out into the middle of the ocean, treading water, head barely above the surface, so I placed an unjustified amount of weight on the experience I shared with him.

Having gone through this experience in an unconscious state, and later becoming conscious, I now see how this behavior, like my tendency to prioritize the needs of others over my own, was part of a much larger pattern. I subconsciously absorbed the very same coping mechanisms that drove my parents into addiction and ultimately led to the dismantling of my family. It is funny how the very behaviors that repel us from our parents so easily become a part of who we are if we do not do the work to acknowledge and heal the pain they caused deep within us. What so easily became a part of my identity did not actually belong to me but was the result of a legacy of pain, without a means of healing, that had been passed down through my DNA. This is something that we must all recognize within ourselves, particularly within the Black community. The trauma of our ancestors is embedded within us, and it is easy to confuse our responses to that trauma with who we actually are. The reality of not knowing who we are beyond that trauma can be frightening, because it may require that we dismantle our entire personality and inadvertently admit that the version of ourselves we have given to the world for however long we have occupied space on this planet may not be who we truly are.

My next relationship began when I was twenty-one and lasted for two years. He was the opposite of everything I had known and exactly what I thought I needed. He was a trainer at a boxing gym in New York, and I was desperately seeking change from the toxic lifestyle I had grown accustomed to. Not long before our relationship began, I was asked to come into my agency for Polaroids and was told that I needed to lose weight if I wanted to continue working. The partying was rapidly catching up to me and my dreams had seemingly been derailed once again because, blinded by the pain, I lost sight of why I moved to New York in the first place. Self-sabotage by means of distraction.

At that point in time, I had not cultivated a level of accountability that would allow me to acknowledge and take responsibility for the choices that led to that particular experience. Naturally, as most do when we are stuck in a victim mentality and induced by a lack of awareness of the power we hold to construct our own reality, I projected the blame outward and made others responsible for how I felt, thus perpetuating the cycle. In hindsight, the trainer was kind but lacked the ability to empathize with me or be a container for my healing. His judgments of others, perhaps cast out of fear of his own shortcomings, prevented me from opening up. I left many parts of my story untold, accentuating certain aspects of my personality while completely disregarding others, so that I might fit into a space that was much too small for me to begin with. I, so badly bruised, gravitated toward his gentleness but never opened up to him about my family, what I'd been through, or who I'd dated before him for fear of scrutiny.

I ended the relationship when I realized that my passion had been extinguished, likely because it hid in the shadows that went unacknowledged. The stagnation and false sense of safety our relationship gave me slowly smothered the fire that once burned inside of me, and I began to hate him for it. His role in my narrative shifted from protagonist to antagonist, as I struggled to maintain a relationship that required me to reject myself for the sake of receiving what I thought was love but could not be because it depended on the suppression of my truth.

To Love Me

I am the daughter of a mother who promised her presence but whose preoccupation with personal pleasure prevented her from filling that space. The daughter of a mother whose absence stung like the frostbitten air of February in Brooklyn whipping across your face. Three hours, 168 miles—the time and space between me and my self-esteem, the time and space between me and my sense of worthiness, the time and space between me and the fantasy I created in my head about what it would be like when she finally made it there, the time and space it would have taken her to keep her word.

I was a child who sat front-row on Greyhound buses every summer when school let out and anxiously, nervously, excitedly, anticipated her mother's arrival. But whose mother could not make it to one dance recital. Back then that three hours seemed like an eternity, and so I empathized, but now I'm a little older and I cannot fathom the thought of three hours keeping me apart from the very thing I gave life to. So if you choose to love me, please know that your actions must match your words. Do not tell me what you are going to do with no intentions of following through; be honest. I will not fault you for being incapable, but please express your limitations so I can adjust my expectations. I live with my heart open and full of hope, and I do not plan on making myself more callous so that it does not hurt as bad when the world lets me down.

If you choose to love me, please know that I am the daughter of a father who struggled to keep the lights on and the water running.

Who drove past the mailbox at the end of our block to avoid opening the bills that were inside because it meant one less confrontation with his pride and one less blow to his ego. Understand that I have made myself small, systematically abandoning my own needs in an effort not to disturb the peace. I was the teenager who started her period and spent an entire summer stuffing tissue into her panties because she knew her father couldn't afford pads. And being the only girl in the house, it seemed liked a selfish thing to even ask for.

So, if you choose to love me, know that I have developed a strong dependency on myself. I have difficulty seeking help. It is hard for me to ask for anything, but I will cherish everything. I do not expect you to read my mind, just please be mindful. As an adult I have learned to reparent myself and accept that a certain degree of selflessness is healthy, but martyrdom serves no one. So, if by the off-chance I do muster up the courage to ask for something, however small it may seem, know that I have had to overcome a great deal of fear to do so, and for me this is a massive accomplishment.

If you choose to love me, please know that, before you, I loved a man who told me to my face my ambition was the reason he couldn't remain faithful. So, when things go wrong, my first instinct is to blame myself and ask what I could have done. I have tried in more ways than one to make myself easy to love. Even if that means staying silent when there are a million words on my mind. I cry more than average but not always from sadness. I am easily overwhelmed and, like a cup that is full to the brim, I cannot contain my emotions. And this is something new for me, something I am proud of, because for a very long time I stopped crying altogether. No one in my life has held space for any emotion other than satisfaction. But I love myself more now than I did back then, and I have given myself the permission that my inner child never had to express how she feels.

I am not difficult, I am human. I ask questions so that I can offer understanding, not to pry, but I cannot offer understanding where communication is never given. If you choose to love me, please know that somehow I have managed to stay open long enough to receive my blessings. I understand that the point of life is change, so rather than placing blame, I am accountable for my actions and constantly extracting lessons so that I can evolve into the best version of me. I am grateful that my reaction to being hurt is no longer further destroying myself. Instead, I offer myself grace and compassion rather than reprimanding. All I ask is that you do the same, if you choose to love me.

Chrysalis

Dear selves

Surrendered to the flow of life
In the presence of love
I remove my disguise
Emotions flood my heart
Tears sting my eyes
I'm reminded of the times
I abandoned myself
Lost the race
Because I forgot I was the prize
Lost my confidence
Because I forgot where God resides
Watched those with whom
I share the same smile
Forfeit their dreams
Boneyards filled with desires

Juxtaposed from justice
Imprisoned in lies
Know now for every trial
Triumph waits on the other side
I thank those who pass judgment
Because I empathize
What pours from my mouth
Is the truth you deny

When I see you

I see me
When I see you
I see me

I am the difference
The ultimate gift
My intuition
Place distance
Between me and those
Who project their limits
Broken mirrors reflect
Unclear visions
Guard my interest
Childlike desires
That make life
Worth living

I can't promise I'll never lose myself again
But I promise I'll keep trying to meet who I'm becoming
I can't promise I'll never lose myself again
But I promise I'll keep trying to meet who I'm becoming

Medicine

What we are truly facing at this time is the extinction of the binary code, a theme that appears in the film *The Matrix* as various sequences of the numbers 1 and 0. Our current reality is programmed according to the binary code, and it shows up in our daily lives as the separation between seemingly opposing forces—male and female, Democrat and Republican, good and evil, Black and white, life and death—in which one force must always be superior to the other. In nature, it is the harmonious union between these seemingly opposite forces which allows for wholeness and fluidity, like the two sides of our brain that do not work in opposition to one another but rather complement one another and work in unison, each serving its own unique purpose.

This unnatural separation has created a dual polarity within the human psyche, which has forced us to highlight the socially acceptable aspects of our personality while suppressing the aspects that push us outside the margins of normality. Not only do we repress the shame, guilt, and trauma we carry for fear of ridicule, but our potential for unique self-expression as well, making it easier for us to be manipulated and controlled. While some of us are more adjusted to the fracturing and splitting of our psyche, which has diminished our power and ability for creativity, those who demonstrate characteristics of what physicians call "bipolar disorder" are often those who can no longer uphold this false binary. Those who are tired of living in opposition to their nature, the truth of who they are. What we have labeled as mental illness is actually the body's natural attempt at mental wellness and wholeness. We simply do not have the awareness in the Western world to recognize it as such. So often everything inside is asking us to do one thing while everything outside is forcing us to do another, and if we do not comply, we become social pariahs, losing opportunities for gainful employment, housing, education, and relationships.

What if we, meaning you and I, were incarnated during this time not to join the system but to destroy it completely? And what is the system? For me, it is the social hierarchy by which certain life-forms are given status and deemed more valuable than others. It is the exploitation of Earth, its resources, and its indigenous people. It is a way of thinking, living, and being that suppresses our true potential as sovereign entities. At least, that is what meets the eye.

Those already doing the intimate work to deconstruct the system and awaken the planet know it is not an external doing but an internal rewriting of one's own programming that alters our collective reality. What if the current social structure is a mere projection of our collective psychological state? It would mean that the state of our society is dictated by the state of the individual, and it is his or her psychological well-being that determines our collective fate.

If one wishes to eradicate the sickness from our planet, they must first work to eradicate the sickness within. Our present system is a virus with which all of us have been deliberately infected. Our identities, the connection we have to our family and community, the foundation of truth upon which we have constructed our lives must all be up for examination and elimination.

The conscious unlearning and reprogramming of my psyche has been my personal work since 2016, after being shaken awake and radicalized by the state-sanctioned murders of Alton Sterling, Philando Castile, and the wave of Black death that preceded theirs. Four years later, we found ourselves in an eerily similar situation following the murders of George Floyd, Breonna Taylor, and Ahmaud Arbery. Shaken out of our collective comatose state in the midst of a global pandemic, forced into our homes, and forced to look within and observe the patterning of our own psyches, unable to distract ourselves with the everyday demands of life. To be alive in 2023 is to not only bear witness but to participate in one of the greatest shifts our planet has yet to undergo. It is time for a quantum leap into the next chapter of our existence. The revolution will not take place in the streets but in the hearts and minds of those ready to free themselves from under the systemic thumb of oppression.

As humans, it is said that for the sake of our sanity one must sometimes dip back into unconscious in order to survive trauma. To behave unconsciously is to behave on autopilot, to follow one's programming without protest. African captives and their descendants have endured generations of trauma and abuse since their abduction, and because of it, we have fallen into a spiritual slumber. It is time for Black people, specifically African American people, to awaken from this slumber and become who we are destined to be and who we have always been. Generations of inherited pain is not an intrinsic part of the human experience, and yet it is the common experience, of all those on the planet right now whose ancestors' bodies were pulled from shores and shipped across the Atlantic Ocean, stacked on top of one another. Our family heirlooms are the scars we wear and the shame we carry, all the memories of our bloodline's suffering imprinted on our DNA, and the sticky residue of slavery still thick in our lungs from the time we take our first breath and cry out for our mothers, who too often die before we ever get a chance to meet them because they are so often neglected. And then we grow into adults who are still unable to breathe. Not with knees in our backs and forearms around our necks and full body weight on our bellies. And now the whole world is sick with this sticky residue and none of us can breathe freely. Without question, survival is in my lineage. It would be a disservice to my ancestors, whose bodies were pulverized under the weight of enslavement, reconstruction, Jim Crow, and centuries of extrajudicial police brutality, to allow this fact to go unrecognized. But be that as it may, for those of us incarnated on Earth at this moment, it is time for us all to do the work to heal ourselves beyond what our ancestors were capable of. We are the ones who carry within us the potential to permanently shift human consciousness, regardless of gender, race, or nationality.

What if the chaos we see before us today is actually a global reestablishment of order, redistribution of power, and realignment with nature? What if living outside of this harmonious balance is the original transgression from which all other acts of evil are born? Imagine perhaps that we are not fighting for the planet, but alongside her, for she is equally outraged, she has been equally brutalized. Even so, it would be foolish and contrary to the laws of nature to parade around as if this beast could be slain without a fight. It isn't going to simply lie down and accept its fate without a final attempt at defending itself. Even if that means being swallowed in a pit of its own flames or devouring itself like a parasite that has grown fat from feasting on everything around it but whose gluttonous appetite won't allow it to stop. An animal is its most dangerous when it is cornered and afraid, hence the current state of our democracy.

* * *

From the time of my conception, it has felt as though there exists an energetic force whose sole mission has been to eradicate me from the planet. Even the primordial waters of my mother's womb could not protect me. At seven months pregnant, the beast struck and the house she was living in was consumed by flames. That burning to the ground of precious possessions that once provided security and comfort would become a metaphor for the remainder of my infancy, childhood, and early adulthood. But all alchemists and scientists know that soot and ash are the most fertile kinds of soil, containing within them all the elements necessary to bring forth new life. Perhaps that same force that could have destroyed me, the energy of four hundred years of slavery and oppression embedded in the cells of my small body, was the same force that awakened me and showed me the way back home to myself. My subconscious patterning, the sum of all my ancestors' pain, showed up in my reality because I was strong enough to face it and transform the energy once and for all so that it will not be inherited by my children.

REACTIVIST (noun)
re·ac·tiv·ist
/ˈrēaktivəst/

Reactivist
Someone who reacts to shit
Pretends to be the protagonist
When really
They setting us backward
Exploiting Black hurt
Profit off of pain
Worse than a greedy pastor
Using every opportunity to broadcast disaster
Using every opportunity to center themselves
Enjoy the clout but don't really help

Woke but not awakened
Book smart but spiritually complacent
Unaware of the real war that we're facing
One that can't be fought with legislation

Your outer world don't change until your inner world changes
Disregard your textbooks they revised all the pages
Can't trust my education 'cause they lie just to tame us and defame us
Desensitized then blame us
Hang us by ropes and maim us
Disfigured by the flame so our bodies remain nameless
Mom staring at the casket can't recognize her own baby

Home of the brave or home of the shameless?
Cop kill my sisters and still walk away blameless
If they can't kill my brothers they gon' throw 'em in cages

Head full of lies got my hair full of lye
But how can I relax when I'm the monster you despise
Goodness of a man gauged by proximity to white
When it's really our darkness which brings forth the light
Turn a Black man into the boogeyman
When it's you, America, who goes bump in the night

Homegrown hate under the guise of apple pies
Strange fruit is in season and the poison is ripe
But I'm hungry for freedom and you can't quell my appetite

I realize that the revolution is inside
And we don't know ourselves so we're easy to misguide

Stuck inside of characters created by our conditioning
Never realize we have a choice in who we get to be

Pick up the pen and rewrite your destiny
Express yourself authentically
Make sure that your choices align with who you're meant to be

Look in the mirror and meet your maker
Your identity's been hijacked and you're your own savior

Surrender the superficial and seek the supernatural
The sun and the stars are ancestors staring at you
I recognize your pain but please recognize your value
They gon' do it long as they can still get a reaction out you

Free your mind to find your sovereign divinity
Integrate your shadow instead of making it your enemy
Tap into duality and recalibrate your energy
Take accountability and search inside for your liberty

Activism

Racial tension was high in the summer of 2016. Alton Sterling, a Black man, had very recently been shot dead at close range by the Baton Rouge police, and Philando Castile, yet another Black man, was murdered on Facebook Live the very next day. All of this just months before the presidential election that would change the course of American history: the election of Donald J. Trump. With social and political circumstances very nearly parallel to those in 2020, and protests erupting in Times Square, public buses hauling away anyone police deemed unlawful or simply chose to target—which did not exclude children and teens—heated tempers flaring up, only exacerbated by the July sun, Black people were yet again forced into a period of collective grief, rage, and hopelessness. Death was on the tips of all our tongues and at the forefront of all our minds.

Earlier that year, I made the choice to begin wearing my natural hair after I started to notice the inception of a natural hair community on social media. For the first time in my life, I saw women with my hair texture wearing various natural styles and discussing products that worked for them. For the first time in my life, I felt as though it was possible for me to wear my hair as it grew out of my head, which at the time was not a symbol of protest but a desperate plea for an ounce of autonomy after years of agents, casting directors, and hairstylists offering opinions, suggestions, and criticisms on the weaves and wigs and clip-in extensions that I wore in an attempt to position myself within the narrow margins of beauty upheld by the fashion industry. And having very little skill or knowledge to support such grandiose egotistical gestures, I suffered at the hands of those who claimed to be experts in their field. I had my body stripped of my genetic inheritance, all in an attempt to achieve some sort of manageable, safe, nonthreatening version of Blackness.

Upon entering my then modeling agency in the spring, hair stretched toward the ceiling rather than relaxed on my shoulders as they had grown accustomed to, I was met with looks of bewilderment and a doubtful curiosity. "What's going on with your hair?" The opening remark catapulted across the room, penetrating my heart, my spine. Waves of anxiousness overwhelming my nervous system. It was not as though I decided to go natural and instantly thought myself to be some Nubian princess with indestructible confidence and an army of ancestors behind her to smite anyone who dare speak out of turn. I was fragile and even more insecure than I had been before, because my security blanket, the thing I believed would keep me safe from the criticism of a world that detests Black women, the thing I had entrusted to open doors for me that I believed my kinky coils could not, was gone. They tried to reason with me. "You will lose the clients you have." "New clients won't want to book you." Threats to my only source of income. A Black girl who had done all she could to break the shackles of poverty, threatened with the idea of having to return to that place with nothing to show for it, for simply wearing her hair as it grows out of her head. To her mother who used her bedroom as a brothel, to her grandmother whose house had become a storage unit for miscellaneous junk. In an instant I saw my life flash before my eyes. It was one thing to be judged, to be talked about, to be berated. Those things hurt, but I could get past them. But being relegated back to destitution seemed such a cruel punishment for simply wanting to be myself. And then the final blow: "That rolled-out-of-bed hair just isn't going to work." I can still hear those words, feel them even, in the exact tone and exact inflection with which they were spoken, like the familiar sting of alcohol on an open wound.

I left my agency that day not only discouraged, but fearful that everything I had worked for would be taken from me. But things could not return to how they had been. The dread and anxiety I faced each day not knowing if the hairstylist would see me as a burden rather than a human; would I be seen as someone who would make their day a little more difficult and tedious? I had held my tongue and my tears too many times before. I craved the freedom to show up in the world as myself; to unapologetically take up space, to use my physical attributes as a means of further expressing the depths of my soul, to jump in a pool or a shower or into life without hesitation, a freedom I had been robbed of for most of my childhood and into adulthood. I was being called toward a higher expression of self, a truer one, and that calling could not be ignored. And my answer to this calling was not without reward. Within three weeks of the interaction I had with my agents, the casting director for Calvin Klein reached out to me directly asking if I would like to be in their upcoming campaign shot by Tyron Lebon in Los Angeles—the biggest opportunity of my career up until that point. In retrospect, I recognize that offer as a universal reaction caused by me stepping further into an authentic expression of self. Truth opens new doors and creates unforeseen possibilities, because it puts us into alignment with our highest potential, and it is our natural attributes that are needed to fulfill this potential. Many people are not in alignment, particularly Black and indigenous people, because we are conditioned to reject those natural attributes.

The idea of perfection, as it stands, is rooted in white supremacy and, therefore, absolutely warped. Striving to reach an ideal that is dictated by man so that one group of people may thrive while all others are oppressed will never breed true joy or satisfaction. Attempting to perfect oneself is an absolute insult to God, an insult to the self, and, furthermore, prevents us from achieving all that we are capable of should we embrace our natural attributes. Rather than striving to become "perfect," our common goal should be to come into alignment with our true nature; to explore our shadows and shamelessly bring forth our talents, creativity, and desires. This is true self-development, and for me, the decision to wear my natural hair was one step in the direction of this authentic self-expression of my true essence.

Shortly after the casting director for Calvin Klein reached out, I was flown to Los Angeles to model in the campaign, and by that summer my face was occupying territory on a billboard in SoHo. The day the campaign went public, I received an email from my agent. The contents: a photo of myself—nostrils wide, lips full, hair defying gravity in all its natural glory—and a message that simply read, "Really proud of you." My heart swelled. I thought back to how hard I had tried to diminish myself to fit a standard that was not for me. I was told that brands only booked Black girls if they looked like they'd been "plucked from a remote village in Africa" or like a "white model dipped in chocolate," and from the start of my career in 2011, I lived by those words, internalizing them, and constantly questioning whether or not I was enough. But this moment defied every last notion of inferiority.

Then, the same day my campaign was released, I found out on Twitter that Alton Sterling had been murdered. I scrolled through a stream of tweets filled with grief, sorrow, anger, and bewilderment until I regrettably found the footage. Heartbreak consumed me; a man's entire existence had once again been reduced to a hashtag. I was on set that day and had to take a break from working, a luxury not afforded to many Black people in times of grief, so that I could allow the emotions that stirred inside of me to solidify into tears, roll down my cheeks, and be released from my body. The source of my tears was unclear. So many thoughts, so many emotions. Years of being turned down, overlooked, and told I wasn't enough of what someone else wanted all led to this moment, and yet, it was in that very same moment that I realized the significance of the Calvin Klein image staring back at me. It is the same lack of value for Black lives that causes Black men and women to be gunned down in the streets without consequence, which also causes Black models to be systematically excluded and disrespected. We don't get the luxury of diverse, carefully thought-out narratives that demonstrate the vast humanity of Black people, only trite stereotypes that perpetuate the idea we are inherently dangerous or criminal.

That evening I went home and began writing an open letter to the fashion industry called "Time For Change," which eventually evolved into a TED talk called "Black Girl Magic in the Fashion Industry" and positioned me as a leading advocate for change within the industry. The open letter elaborated on the correlation between the lack of value for Black lives in fashion and social justice and made a plea to the fashion industry to be more inclusive in order to "neutralize the phobias surrounding Black culture rather than perpetuating trite stereotypes that vilify people of color." Less than twenty-four hours later I checked my news feed again, only to find that yet another Black man had been killed by the police.

Desensitized

I'm desensitized
So I let the sentence cry
Sympathy incentivized by likes
And massacres televised
News cycles, new lies
Media angles weaponized
Terrorized
But never tears in eyes

Too many coffins
Too much
Too often
This shit is exhausting
Every day
More losses
System won't change
Life not worth what it cost them
Enough thoughts and prayers
To turn heaven into a mosh pit
All just hot air
Inflated sense of Godship

I'm desensitized
Like I've been robbed
Of tongue, ears, and eyes
How human am I?

Still fuck the police
But my emotions are hog-tied

Another victim slain
Feels like novocaine to me
Heart won't let me feel
Only guilt from apathy
Empathy their enemy
2020 couldn't breathe
Still gasping for air
As far as eye can see

Time For Change

An Open Letter to the Fashion Industry
as published by *Harper's Bazaar*

Last week, I received an email from my agent at MC2 Model Management. The contents: a photo of myself—nostrils wide, lips full, hair defying gravity in all its natural glory—in Calvin Klein's Fall 2016 campaign and a message that simply read, "Really proud of you." My heart swelled. I thought back to how hard I had tried to assimilate into the fashion industry—straightening my hair, wearing weaves and extensions. I was told that brands only booked Black girls if they looked like they'd been "plucked from a remote village in Africa" or like a "white model dipped in chocolate," and from the start of my career in 2011, I lived by those words. Until last year when I made the decision to wear my natural hair.

That same day, Twitter informed me that Alton Sterling, a Black man, had been shot and killed by the police. I scrolled through a stream of tweets filled with grief, sorrow, anger, and bewilderment until I regrettably found the footage of his murder. Heartbreak instantly consumed me; a man's entire existence had once again been reduced to a hashtag. Less than twenty-four hours later I checked my news feed again, only to find that yet another Black man had been killed by the police.

It was only then that I realized the importance of the Calvin Klein image staring back at me. As artists in the fashion industry, we are the embodiment of free speech. We set the tone for society through the stories we tell—fashion, the gatekeeper of cool, decides and dictates what is beautiful and acceptable. And let me tell you, it is no longer acceptable for us to revel in Black culture with no regard for the struggles facing the Black community.

Every year, particularly during fashion week, there is an outcry felt throughout the industry. From the disproportionately low number of models of color walking in the shows (Blacks make up less than 10 percent of models on the runway; models of color make up 24.75 percent), to the lack of makeup artists trained to work on colored skin; from the mismatching of foundation to the burning and ripping out of hair. We sit in silence for fear of being labeled "a diva" while being inflicted with pain, or watching our faces turn grey.

With greater frequency, we've experienced an uproar of outcry in regard to the deaths of Black men at the hands of police officers. The correlation? Inequity. It is the same systemic racism that sees beauty products for "Black" hair end up in a section of their own ("the ethnic aisle"), that sees Black men more likely to end up dead after a police encounter than any other racial group. Systemic racism began with slavery and has woven itself into the fabric of our culture, manifesting through police brutality, poverty, lack of education, and Black incarceration. The most dangerous contributors? Advertising, beauty, and fashion.

We must band together to neutralize the phobias surrounding Black culture. Rather than perpetuating trite stereotypes that vilify people of color, we need to produce positive, accurate, and inclusive imagery. My advice to makeup and hair artists: rebuild your repertoire of techniques. My advice to models, fashion designers, and public relations agencies: use your personal platforms to speak out against injustice and show your support rather than standing by in silence. Most importantly, love Black people as much as you love Black music and Black culture. Until you do, society will continue to buy into the false notion that people of color are less than—a concept already deeply embedded in America's collective psyche, which is reinforced again and again through depictions in media. The time for change is now.

I Live in a Different World

I live in a different world
My own world
It is gorgeous and ripe
But it is also lonely
I have extended invitations before
Some politely decline
Most just don't understand

At times I wish to leave this world
To dwell in the common reality
But I am not able
It is beautiful and frightening
It is love and hate
It is everything and nothing
It is isolation and great company
It is within me and around me
It is God
And it is mine

Awakening

As I sat, perched on my bed, a week after having written my open letter to the fashion industry, midday summer sunlight seeping through the half-open window shades in my Brooklyn bedroom, and eyes glazed over from scrolling through my social media feed, I caught a glimpse of a man who I would come to know, quickly grow to love, and eventually toward whom I would feel nothing at all. The image was captured by a photographer friend of mine who had a knack for skillfully illuminating brown skin and its heavenly radiance. The photo that caused me to focus my ever-softening vision and readjust my resting limbs so as to better digest what appeared on the small screen before me was no exception. He was gorgeous. His skin was dark Black, his smile was bright white, and his charisma dripped from the photograph like water from a sink with a slow leak—so much certainty in his expression. In an instant, I was captivated and determined to figure out who he was. Naturally, I tested the waters by first liking the photograph, nothing over the top or too direct, and to my surprise and great pleasure he liked one back and began following me. Soon we were exchanging numbers, texting, calling, and FaceTiming daily.

With social unrest as the backdrop to our narrative, this man I met on social media and I naturally found ourselves engulfed in conversations on the topic of Black liberation and what it meant to truly be free, each conversation lasting for hours. We talked Baldwin and Maya, Angela and Huey. Lauryn, Erykah, Kanye, and Nipsey. But most important we talked about God. Not the God who injected us with guilt and shame. Not the God whom I had loved as a child but resented as an adult who could see how the church only perpetuated her father's depression. This God did not decorate the pulpit and the stained-glass windows. This God decorated the walls of my heart—this God was alive inside of me.

Although our bond was never physical, it was intense. The passion I felt toward him consumed my entire being. His words were poetry. His self-expression awakened what had been sleeping inside of me for over two decades. It was as if God himself had entered the body of this mortal man to call me back home. I was waking up to my truth—self-love, authenticity, freedom from social identity—and he was the alarm clock. He'd ask, "What does it look like to love yourself?" and "What personal truths would you share to save others from suffering alone?" Seeds in the form of questions that he planted in my psyche, still reverberating through my conscious to this day. But he did not stay around long enough to harvest the fruit. Despite its depth, our connection was fleeting. What had been an endless stream of messages and phone calls back and forth slowed to a trickle and then dried up completely. What had once quenched a thirst that I had no awareness of prior to his arrival was suddenly gone. I felt abandoned, and once again I was face-to-face with one of my deepest, most ancient wounds. I put him on a pedestal where I could no longer see his humanity. I could not recognize his shortcomings, nor could I gauge his fears. I could only see his perfection. And I, with awareness of all my imperfections, could only blame myself for his disappearance.

The truth was, I wish I'd made it through the trauma of my youth unscathed, but that was simply not the case. The truth was, no matter how much I transformed or transcended or achieved, remnants of my past remained. The truth was, I contracted the herpes virus at eighteen years old while dating my first boyfriend, and until that point, the only people who knew were myself and God. I did not blame him for his disappearance, and yet it hurt just the same. I was rejected for the very same truth he provoked. The truth he emboldened me to finally hold up to the light of day and examine with clear eyes. The truth that I thought would set me free.

Some avoid their lessons by refusing to accept and operate within their truth, while others, like myself, become the teacher of them. But the lesson I have learned, and therefore the lesson I teach, is not what one might assume. We are all plenty familiar with safe sex discourse. What I have learned is that the difference between a wound and a scar is the examination of it, and the subsequent healing that has taken place. The changes that have been implemented. The recognition that has been given. The forgiveness that has been offered. The self-love that has been cultivated. To some those scars will be unattractive, undesirable, maybe even repulsive. But to others, they will be enticing—not in a voyeuristic way, but in a way that provokes genuine curiosity. They will find them interesting, brave, heroic, and worthy of praise. In many ways it has preserved me, kept me from opening myself up to those who I knew did not have the capacity to hold my naked truth but desired to hold my naked body.

There is a fine line between a gift and a curse, and that line is called perspective. Through the elevation of my perspective and by bearing witness to the patterns of my own life, I recognize that the darkest parts of my past are a gateway to the brightest parts of my future, and what some might consider a thorn to their flesh actually fortified me. I have not been taken off course by distractions, worldly attachments, or relationships of no significant value. Nor have I made it anyone's responsibility other than my own to discover and replenish what I lacked. I have been purposefully positioned in this lifetime to cultivate a level of self-love and discipline that has lent itself to the veneration, vindication, and purification of my entire bloodline. I have been obedient, steadfast, and intentional with the time I have been given. I have become an extraordinary truth-teller, breaking through shame and taboo for the sake of healing, inspiring, and liberating as many souls as God will allow me to touch. I have rediscovered my self-worth and have decided that I am deserving of my own admiration. And whoever chooses to offer me love outside of my own, will serve to overflow a cup that is already filled to the brim.

Although the outcome was outside of my expectation, my truth did set me free. In fact, I am freer than most, because I do not deny myself; I do not shun myself. I do not need to search outside of myself for acceptance, because there is no part of myself that I do not accept; therefore, I do not depend on the approval of others for validation. I sleep well at night knowing that I have confirmed the health and sought forgiveness from those to whom my truth was not afforded for fear of rejection and that my karmic debt has been paid. I do not consider what if, only what is, and what is are these words on these pages, in this chapter, bound by this book, that are setting somebody free in this very moment. We do not always get to choose our truth, but we do get to decide how we use or misuse it. The truth can be a prison cell, or it can be the key that opens your cage and the cages of everyone around you.

Although I have suffered greatly, I remind myself that I will only be here for a short while. One hundred years, if I am lucky. But the truth that I administer will be medicine for many lifetimes beyond my own. And the healing I confront will extend many lifetimes before. Just like the pyramids house the truths of the ancient Egyptians, my heart houses a timeless truth that not only belongs to me but to all of humanity, for it has the power to purify and liberate not only my bloodline, but the bloodlines of countless others for generations to come.

Regardless of the fact that I had never felt a pain more excruciating than that feeling (like I had just lost the person I was certain I would spend the rest of my life with), I now understand why God had to do this. It was an invitation to come back home to myself. It was not him that I truly desired, but all of the qualities that lay dormant within me that he mirrored back. And how could I be a mirror to someone else if I was too afraid to face myself?

After communication dried up, I convinced myself that if I could become more like him, then he would eventually see me, love me, choose me, but every encounter only led to deeper rejection. However, in the process of striving to be desired by him, I began to desire myself more deeply than ever before. The constant rejection forced me to choose myself time after time instead of giving my power away and hoping that another would fill the void of the love I deprived myself of. I came to realize that I felt abandoned by him only because I had made a habit of abandoning myself, which I first learned from my mother, then again from my father, then again from lovers. He was showing me, me.

I believed my benevolence, generosity, and kindness was a character trait that meant I was strong and capable of love despite a lack of reciprocity, but really it was the product of pain, a pattern that I created to ensure my needs would be met, making myself not only useful but boundary-less and self-sacrificing in exchange for love and attention. The truth is, I needed to chase him, and he needed to reject me, so that I could stop rejecting myself—so I could stop putting him and others on pedestals and start to embody the very qualities that attracted me to him in the first place. He was not sent to be my life partner but to free me and eventually trigger me so deeply that I'd have no choice but to transform, and for that I am grateful.

But before I became aware, I first became destructive. I did not understand why God would put me through such pain. I spent time in a hell of my choosing. I surrounded myself with people whose pain mirrored my own and whose vices kept me numb. The cycle of destruction was familiar, almost comfortable. Except this time, a glimmer of consciousness. A sense of purpose. A connection with the divine that I did not have before. As time passed and my consciousness grew, I began to recognize this cycle of self-destruction and became angry. I blamed those who I had once considered friends for pulling me out of alignment with my truth. I was filled with resentment. I felt as though I had been tricked and led down a path that was not mine to walk. But then, with even greater consciousness, the awareness that my choices made me complicit in my own suffering, and that only I could save myself, I began to discover the true meaning of accountability.

Most Days

I've been mourning
For three years now.
I don't know when death
Became my closest companion
But she shows up for me
Often.
She comes for me
With a raging fire,
Ready to burn up
Anything that doesn't align
With the most authentic
Expression of myself:
Love.

I've lost many versions of myself
To this ruthless flame.
I've lost friendships,
Relationships, and
Connections.
I've been stripped down,
Emptied, and
Laid bare.
Everything I once believed
To be a part of me,
Everything that I ever loved,
Has been burned up in the fire—

Lost in the magic.
The pain of hitting rock bottom
Awakened me to my own power
And I've been trying to save myself
Ever since.
I've peeled away layers of myself
That I believed
Were intrinsically part of me
Only to discover
They were borrowed.

I've tormented myself,
Desperate to take those I love
On a journey
That was only meant
For me;
Never realizing
How unfair it was
To expect
Them to keep my pace.
How could I expect them
To submit to death
With the same readiness?

How could I expect
Their willingness to endure
A pain that I
Have not yet found

A remedy for?
Nobody teaches you
How to manage
The grief
That comes with transcending
Identity
Or how to navigate
The world
Without a predetermined
Sense of belonging.
Nobody teaches you
How to deal with
The suffering
That comes with
Evolving
Within a society
That thrives off
Mediocrity
And repression.

Nobody teaches you
How to create
Your own patterns,
Standards,
And ideals
Rather than adopting
And settling for
A life based on

Cultural norms.
Out here
Nothing makes sense;
Only the sense
You create for yourself.
It's all too big,
Amorphous,
Nonlinear,
Infinite.

At times I feel seen,
Heard,
Felt,
Understood.

Then I'm reminded
That for many
I will never be more
Than a projection,
A mirror,
Reflecting an uncomfortable truth.

That they have been living life
Below their full potential.
That their identity-centric existence
Has limited them.
That they live a life of servitude—

Slaves to a fear
That has no basis in reality.
For this reason
They will never see me
Let alone
Love me.

Most days
I'm okay with that.
Most days
I'm at peace.
Most days.

The Quest for Black Christ

The word *archetype* can be broken down into two parts. *Arche* meaning "source of action" and *type* meaning "to have common characteristics." Archetypes are psychological energy patterns that humans have embodied throughout history across all cultures and ethnicities.

For example, Oshun, Isis, Parvati, Aphrodite, and Venus are deities throughout history who span many cultures yet embody the same archetype: the lover. Even the planet Venus has been personified and endowed with these particular characteristics. The practice of astrology seeks to use the individual characteristics assigned to each planet as a rubric for understanding our own psychological structures. We are able then to become conscious of how the placement and movement of each planetary body plays out in our daily lives within our relationships, family dynamics, and on a larger scale within our social and political structures.

To understand this process, we must first understand light and sound as the fundamental building blocks of our universe. When these waves of light and sound enter our psyche, vibrating at various frequencies, they shape our individual and collective experiences. It is believed that all matter is wave before it is particle.

Real change occurs at the fundamental level when our psyche becomes aligned with a particular energy pattern or wave form, which then informs our master value system or belief system. We go forward making choices that support this belief system, and those choices become the fabric of our reality. These psychological changes, if made on a large scale, have the power to completely reshape society. However, we only have a finite amount of space within our psyche, so we must rid ourselves of previously held values so that they can be replaced or updated by new ones. If your body is the hardware, then your value system is the software. You have to delete old apps so you can download new ones.

Once our value system is in alignment with the values of a particular archetype, we are able to integrate it and embody it. Essentially, we have the power to rewrite our personal DNA, which itself is a sequence of patterns, through the embodiment of preexisting energy patterns. This newly embodied energy pattern gives your DNA instructions on how to write and replicate itself according to who you wish to become rather than who you have been. It is an opportunity for the ultimate identity switch.

What would Jesus do? Asking oneself this question is an example of how those who wish to integrate and embody the energy of Jesus Christ might go about rearranging their value system. When we read the Bible, the words carry a vibration that penetrates our psyche and rearranges our value system to be in alignment with that of God and Christ. I believe that Jesus Christ was the physical incarnation of spiritual perfection, vibrating on the frequency of Love, which is the highest in our universe. His existence set a precedent and created a blueprint for all those coming after to strive for. Furthermore, I believe that mass achievement of this frequency of Love will be the spur that propels humanity and Earth into the next iteration of our evolution.

"Fake it 'til you make it" is another way of saying, embody the value system of the person you wish to become until you integrate that energy pattern into your DNA, which will express itself in your personality and way of being.

Personally, I no longer wish to be called an activist, because I feel my identity has transcended the need for labels, but at one point, it was essential that I embody the activist archetype so that I could fulfill my purpose. More commonly known in archetypal studies as The Warrior, "activist" was the label I took on while studying the value system of those throughout history who embodied the same energy, such as Angela Davis and Huey P. Newton.

We subconsciously undergo this process while listening to music. That's why artists like Tupac Shakur and Nipsey Hussle, with their radicalized messages, seemed larger than life. With their values so clearly vocalized, we were able to embody their energy, expanding the field of their individual consciousness by absorbing it into our collective consciousness. Nipsey himself said that he looked to Tupac as an example of someone who embodied the same energy that he would later come to embody on his own quest to become Christlike.

Undoubtedly, it is much easier to embody these archetypal energy patterns when they are presented in the form of deities, heroes, and rap artists rather than complex genetic codes, and easier still when those deities and heroes look like you. However, in our present culture ruled by its lust for power (or what we perceive as power), celebrity worship, and white supremacy, our ancient deities have been appropriated, white-washed, or completely forgotten about. Our heroes have been written out of history and our rappers have been stripped of substance. Thus, we have collectively aligned our individual values with those who are simply popular, wield political power, have a lot of money, or uphold widely accepted standards of beauty and living. Therein lies the danger of not being completely conscious of what you consume; eventually, it becomes your programming.

During my years as a social media user, I've felt a silent pull to conform to particular standards of beauty, fashion, and fitness, and it has only increased in intensity as algorithms become a more prominent feature of these apps. Through carefully curated photos, we have created an alternate reality where only the most ideal and palatable versions of ourselves can exist. But this behavior has real-world repercussions. Culturally, we are becoming dangerously homogeneous: afraid of expressing our individuality and instead living our lives for the approval of others. This fear of judgment has made conformity the norm and authenticity elusive. How well we market ourselves on virtual platforms now informs the way we date, who we befriend, and who we hire for jobs. It has completely changed how we see others and, moreover, how we see ourselves.

If we do not take dominion over our individual value systems, our programming will be written by those who perpetuate the dominant narrative through stereotyping (which is indisputably a method of brainwashing), social media, popular music, and a twenty-four-hour news cycle, which regurgitates the same stories with the same caricatures day-in and day-out as a means of upholding the current social order. Without a sovereign and intentionally constructed value system, we will inevitably find ourselves stuck inside these caricatures, equipped with socially engineered personalities, allowing our individual identities to be hijacked by those who aim to push their agenda.

Since every interaction we have with the outside world is dictated by our individual value system, if we are programmed with the value system of those in control of the dominant narrative, we will take action according to their beliefs rather than our own. Their beliefs will then show up in our personalities, our family dynamics, our relationships, our interactions with friends and coworkers, and our political and religious views, thus feeding their power by enslaving ourselves within the social hierarchy. Racism, sexism, and ableism, for example, are not only products of the current social order, they are the fuel required to power it.

That is why nuanced representation and diverse storytelling is imperative. As the old adage goes, "You cannot be what you cannot see." Culturally, we, as Black people, have been blinded to our own greatness for far too long. We must become the authors of our own destiny, and, in order to do so, we must be the authors of our past and present. We must be the ones to tell the stories of our great leaders and changemakers so that they are not written into history as passive, amicable alliances of the state, as they are in the writing of Western history. We must get curious about our gods, our goddesses, our kings, our queens, our warriors, our orishas, our healers, our artists, our activists, our ancestors, and the legacies of those who came before us who were catalysts for great change. We must break free from the system through the conscious unbecoming of Western caricatures and stereotypes and the becoming of heroes and deities, for this is our true identity.

Black Is

Against all odds
We made it through ashes
To be reborn as gods
There is no adversity we cannot withstand
I guess that makes me Superwoman
And you Superman
Heavenly hues dictate the landscape
Upon which this nation stands
That means our collective fate
Is in your Black hands
You hold the key to the kingdom
You are the power
The evil shall be devoured
The meek shall reign
The divine shall be showered
May we receive our flowers
Before we lie in caskets
May we relinquish the backhanded tactics
Preventing us from knowing we are magic
May the world understand
Just how poetic Black is

Butterfly

Accountability

We don't know accountability
Only quick fixes
And temporary pleasure
To distract our senses
We only know pointing the finger
Never at ourselves and always at another
Never stop to wonder
Why the cycles seem relentless
Wash rinse repeat
I've had enough of dirty dishes
It's like we've come to a consensus
Forfeit our power and
Let dictators make decisions
Like them same motherfuckers
Ain't the reason for the sickness
Like them same motherfuckers
Ain't have your daddy in prison
And your mother crying 'cause
She can't afford gifts on Christmas
Like them same motherfuckers
Ain't have Assata on a hit list
I'm saying
Why you trust this system
Over trusting yourself?
Like a politician give a fuck
Like they really here to help
Been sitting in shit so long

You done lost your sense of smell
'Cause this shit here really hell
And only you can save yourself
But all that shame and guilt
Make you pretend you someone else
Reject your skin, nose, hair,
Now you can't access inner wealth
Pain in your veins and
All it wants is to be felt
I rather make my own footprints
Than to follow the same trail
Surrendered your sovereignty
No faith in a higher self
Still you place
Full faith in an election
Lesser of two evils
But the wound is festering
Political gestures
Turn Black folks to jesters
What good is a Tubman
When the cut is infected
America been sinning
It's time for karma collection
I say let the bitch burn
Let's plant seeds in the ashes
This system obsolete
Stop tryna hold on to the past when
A new world's being born
These are the contractions

Transformation

Accountability made everything clearer but nothing easier, and by twenty-four I knew a part of me needed to "die." Like the caterpillar, I died over and over until the life I knew was nothing more than a distant memory. It became evident to me that I was an instigator of my own suffering and I, with my newfound sense of accountability, had to take ownership over it all. I could no longer play the victim, that was not my story anymore. I was too self-aware. It was my own choices that misled me. It was my absence of boundaries that allowed my energy to be siphoned and taken advantage of by those who occupied space in my life and facilitated my erosion. It was my lack of self-love that blinded me to my inherent value and kept me entrapped in cycles of destructive behavior, living below my full potential.

Over and over, my soul asked me to surrender—to sever connections that were energetically draining, to break habits and alter behaviors that no longer served me, to make choices that were in alignment with the person I wanted to become, to release an identity that I had known my entire life—and whenever I resisted these changes and held on to what was so familiar to me, I was dragged until I finally let go. The pain of this death was even more unrelenting than the pain of heartbreak, and its effects were physical. At times, I couldn't sleep, and other times, I could not wake up. My appetite was irregular. My skin broke out. The lymph nodes under my arms became inflamed and filled with pus. I cried every day for months. My body was releasing, rejecting who and what I had been. I was alone in solitude. Suicidal ideation became a regular occurrence. I spent time imagining what it would be like to just disappear for a while, so I would no longer have to face myself and deal with the embarrassment and shame that haunted me. I died a thousand deaths. I died until there was nothing left of me. And it is from this nothingness, from this state of utter humility, that I realized I had the potential to become anything.

At twenty-five I became my own hero. I completely gave up the idea that someone or something outside of me could rescue me from my reality and, instead, started loving myself in a way that transformed it. I buried the corpses of past selves so that flowers could grow in their place. I gave birth to an entirely new version of myself, whose personality and behaviors were not a product of expectations, trauma, or social conditioning, but a product of choice. I began to consciously reconstruct my way of being by reprogramming what I believed about myself. For too long, I lived my life stuck inside of a character whose actions were dictated by the story I was born into, and for too long, that story informed my sense of worthiness and capability. Only by becoming aware of my ability to reprogram my own mind was I able to experience the freedom and power of stepping outside of that story and into one where I was consciously writing my own script, casting the characters, and creating my own destiny. I did not know I wasn't free until I tasted this freedom and, once I tasted it, my appetite became insatiable. But one question still remained: If I was not who I believed myself to be for all those years, if my identity was not determined by race, gender, occupation, sexual orientation, the family I was born into, the community I was raised in, or anything that happened to me in my past, then who was I?

It was this lingering question that, in 2018, led me to West Africa and inspired me to found my nonprofit organization Daughter Org, which provides birthright trips for descendants of the continent to return home for life-changing immersive experiences. It was also this lingering question, in tandem with my ever-expanding awareness, that led me to make a remarkable discovery: That without attachment to any one particular identity or the limitations of labels and rigid social expectations, it was and is entirely up to me to decide who I am and what I am capable of. Without attachment to the version of myself that was produced in response to the world around me, I am boundless in my self-expression. I am an infinite expression of God's love, from which I am not separate but intrinsically linked. And my vessel, which dictates how the world sees me or does not see me, and for so long dictated how I saw myself, is not who I truly am. It is merely a conduit through which I am able to access and channel infinite creative energy so that I may reshape the world around me according to the will of the one consciousness which connects all living things. To recognize myself as a manifestation of this consciousness and surrender to the source energy that is within me and within all of us is to genuinely know true freedom.

The Final Hour

Crystal blue waters
And majestic landscapes
Raising sons and daughters
Freedom can't be taken away
Give thanks to the Earth
Who birthed our tribe
Give thanks to the mothers
Who birth new life
Honor the men
Who protect our pride
Respect the inner child
Where our innocence
Comes alive

So often we take from others
What we lack within
Detached from the source
Where abundance is infinite
Our cups are empty yet
We give and we give
Until there's nothing left
Just left with the resentment

Striving to reach goals
Not our own
But of another man's choosing

Illusions of success so
Happiness is never the conclusion
Creative gifts exploited
By the system
Cause confusion
Deceived by delusion

Desensitized to what it means
To truly be human
Consumed by our greed
In this game we're all losing
Divest from the system
And move with love to
Improve it

Now is the time to awaken
Our true power
Fortify your spirit
For this is the final hour

Transcendence

What if the election of Donald J. Trump was a cosmic attempt at bringing to light the evils embedded within the American subconscious so that we may do the work to eradicate it? What if this virus, the sickness permeating our culture, is our own consciousness pushed out from the psychological into the physical? I encourage you to look beyond what you think is happening, to see what is really going on. To see that this is not a time for panic or chaos, but an invitation to evolve beyond our present way of being into a way of being that is in alignment with nature and does not oppress, suppress, or suffocate the life out of us. The cure to this sickness is not a simple vaccine; that is the equivalent of putting a bandage over a gaping, infected wound. In order to reach a place of true healing and harmony, we must completely expose the sickness and confront its cause. We must be willing to ask questions and come face-to-face with the answer. It is absolutely imperative to realize that each and every one of us is responsible for cleaning up the mess we are in, starting first with ourselves.

If we truly wish to transcend the energetic imprint of slavery, we must acknowledge that emotions are actual things with actual form—charges of energy with their own density that occupy space. And if we do not face them and feel them, they do not leave our bodies. They are forced, over and over, to one region of the body, where they build and compound, causing blockages to that area and preventing the flow of energy necessary to remain in good health. That is how diseases like cancer are created; the repeated stress of unfelt emotions shoved down into one small corner of the body decade after decade, century after century, lifetime after lifetime.

Starting in my early twenties, around the same time I went through my first heartbreak, I began experiencing severe cramps during my menstrual cycle, which by my mid-twenties evolved into unbearable pain. This pain kept me ill throughout my cycle, preventing me from performing even the simplest of tasks. I'd lay for hours, hunched over with tears streaming down my face, unable to eat or drink because the consumption would induce nausea and eventually it would come right back up.

I now know that the persistent pain I'd experienced during my menstrual cycle was due to the unfelt emotions, and, therefore, the unexpressed energy I had buried deep down into that small area of my body. Due to the nature of my mother's work, I had been exposed to so much adult activity as a child, without the maturity to make sense of the feelings it provoked, and the constant stimulation completely overwhelmed my nervous system. The sounds of adult pleasure, the photographs, the magazines, the toys, the tapes—I felt the energy of it all around me and absorbed it into my infant body, where it was met by centuries of sexual trauma faced in lifetimes before my own.

During my healing process, I was forced to revisit every instance of shock, embarrassment, shame, and guilt that I pushed inside of my uterus from infancy, and to feel it all so that it could be released, and I could be set free. Every tear unshed, every word unspoken, every moment that I wanted to call out but was forced to hold my tongue, every moment I did call out and my cries went untended to. The neglect, the hunger, the needs unmet, I had to feel it all. And not from the perspective of the adult who pitied the child, but from the perspective of the child who held on so tightly as the world around her spun too fast.

I am certain I would have developed some form of cancer had I not come to this understanding at such an early age. So many of my friends of a similar age have had invasive operations on their reproductive systems to combat fibroids, cysts, polyps, and other growths. Still, the medical industrial complex claims they have no explanation for this phenomenon or why it is more common in Black women, aside from what they have quietly admitted regarding the use of perms and relaxers and how they are directly linked to reproductive devastation. The only other explanation given is that they just "show up" and nothing can be done to prevent their development or stop their return. Before coming into full consciousness that the root cause of my persistent menstrual pain was emotional blockages, I too underwent surgery. Not only did I put my body through yet another traumatic experience, making myself vulnerable to our historically negligent healthcare system, I felt no relief during the menstrual cycles that followed. After years of suffering and pleading with God for solutions, I put all my faith into this procedure, only to be left devastated.

As descendants of enslaved African women, we carry the sexual trauma of four-hundred-plus years in our wombs. It's no secret that, as African people, we have a natural sensual quality about us; it is in our DNA, and it is the lifeline that connects us back to the source. Our captors knew this about us, and they used it against us. All the times we were raped and forced to remain silent. All the times we had to watch our men raped and broken. All the times we had to watch our children raped and not be allowed to shed a single tear on their behalf without consequence. All the experiments done on our bodies for the sake of medical advancement. All the forced hysterectomies. All the fraudulent abortions. All the unmedicated pain under the false notion that Black women don't feel. For centuries, rape was used as a primary weapon of war against African people, the same way disease was used as a primary weapon of war against the Natives, and all the emotions these experiences conjured up still live inside our bodies.

Never before have we had the luxury or even the safety to feel those emotions. All we've known for so long is survival, which has only served to add more trauma to the pain already dwelling inside of us. We use IUDs, pain killers, and birth control to keep up with the demands of capitalism, while neglecting the true source of our pain. We allow ourselves to be gaslit and called crazy while suffering from PMS because we do not understand our menstrual cycles as an opportunity to purge stagnant emotions. We have forgotten that, like all other pain, this is an invitation to change, to heal. It is our body's attempt to aid us in this healing, but instead of acknowledging, honoring, and releasing the emotions that arise, we resent them and medicate them into submission.

Because we are not educated on the emotional and spiritual functions of our menstrual cycle, we do not utilize Earth's ability to transmute those stagnant emotions into something beautiful and powerful. Instead, we menstruate directly into the water systems of cities that have the technology to sanitize the water but do not have the technology to filter out the energetic debris that is being released. No different from the water in our cells, the water in these systems holds the memory of this energetic imprint. So we drink and bathe in each other's sickness.

As a people, we have lost the true meaning of self-care. Black women, in particular, have grown so accustomed to caring for everyone else that they have systematically overlooked and disregarded their own needs. Worse, they have used this care for others as a cloak to disguise the ways in which patriarchy and white supremacy have penetrated their own psyches. Justifying their toxic behavior under the guise of victimhood from all the abuse they have suffered. No doubt they are indeed victims of this abuse, but liberation is only possible once we cease to forfeit accountability for our actions. It must be understood that patriarchy and capitalism do not just make predators out of men; they make predators out of women as well.

In my life, I have heard countless stories of men who were raped or molested by older women, sometimes even family members, but deceived into believing that it was some sort of initiation into manhood, a badge of honor that should be worn with pride. And upon brief examination of our society today, you will see the precise result of deceiving young boys into believing that their manhood is intrinsically linked to sexual conquest. In tandem, they are fed images of masculinity centered around violence toward women and, even more frequently, toward one another. And when a boy or young man cannot live up to this warped concept of masculinity, he is shunned by the men in his life who have successfully taken on the lie. But when he does live up to it, instead of being loved, he is feared and despised by the victims of his programming. And that external rejection of this pseudo-masculinity, over time, becomes an internal rejection of authentic masculinity.

Our men are hurting—they are in a great deal of pain because they don't have the privilege of identifying as victims, which would, at the very least, give context to their experiences and allow permission for them to seek help. Instead, they are told they must endure this abuse without question, and that speaking out about this great injustice makes them less of a man. Because women do not have the same physical strength, men are often left confused about their experiences of rape and molestation, and basic statistics point to the manifestation of this unexpressed pain, confusion, and shame in men's bodies, as well. Prostate, an organ of the male reproductive system, is the most common type of cancer men develop.

Robbed of their innocence at such a young age, their souls and psyches become fractured, and they unknowingly live their entire lives in pursuit of wholeness. Masking their emptiness in achievements and material gain, taking from others what they feel they no longer possess: their autonomy. Thus, creating a never-ending cycle of abuse. Taking sex from women, dating younger women whom they can easily manipulate, and, at worst, harming children.

Oppositely, this cycle of abuse works no different for women. Robbed of their innocence at a young age, they subconsciously seek out broken partners, traumatized children concealed in the skin of grown men's bodies, whom they can easily manipulate. Or they, still children themselves in their late teens or early twenties, engage with boys much younger, because it was done to them. As older women, they whisper sly comments without repercussion: "You're so handsome, just like your daddy." And just like men, at its worst manifestation, when the appetite for innocence can no longer be met by these subtle energetic exchanges, they begin going after children. And for both genders, all the shame, abuse, guilt, and confusion compounded in the genital area, is pushed down and met with the shame, abuse, guilt, and confusion of four hundred years, lowering our body's energetic frequency and making us a vibrational match for illnesses such as endometriosis and cancer and sexually transmitted diseases, such as HSV2, HIV, and AIDS.

Substances such as alcohol, processed foods, psychoactive government-distributed marijuana, prescription pills—which are highly marketed to the Black community through pop culture—and harmful chemicals—which are highly marketed to Black women by the beauty and cosmetic industry—only exacerbate this issue. Lowering our body's frequencies and making us susceptible to penetration by low vibrating entities that cause illness. Why do you think liquor is called spirits? Why do we awaken from evenings of heavy drinking to hear stories of ourselves acting so out of character that we can hardly accept it as truth? Many of us are possessed by low vibrating entities or "spirits" that have taken up residence in our bodies in reaction to the trauma we have faced. Our lower frequency emotions, such as embarrassment and regret, make us vulnerable to these low frequency entities, and our media only serves to perpetuate this hijacking of our mental and physical wellness. Our own celebrities are often used to market this poison to us and further destroy our community.

When you look around at the fashion, entertainment, and music industries, it becomes quite obvious that our bodies are still being commodified and exploited for the personal gain of those in power. Why is it that what's popular is always sexy and provocative but intelligence and modesty are rarely ever exemplified? This constant intentional exemplification of sex is a form of psychological warfare that affects us all, but especially children.

From personal childhood experience, I have learned that the crossing and overlooking of children's boundaries, even as it pertains to the media they consume, is indistinguishable to the psyche from sexual abuse. Yet we collectively behave as if children have no agency over their bodies. We treat them like possessions; therefore, they become possessed by the same energies that control us. Trauma isn't always caused by a painful experience. Often, it is caused by an experience we simply don't have the language or maturity to understand. If the system can successfully traumatize a child by the time they have reached their teenage years by exposing them to adult content before they are equipped with the maturity to decipher their emotions, they have already weakened the child's immunity to these entities. Many of us, especially descendants of enslaved people, are already born with so much pain, that these entities are latched on to us before we ever even see the light of day.

These entities have attachments to our bloodline that have existed for hundreds or even thousands of years.

The evil forces of the world know this to be true, so they only give visibility to that which suits their brainwashing agenda. Listen to the mainstream music, observe the mainstream artists, watch the popular movies. The agenda is hidden in plain sight, and we ingest it willfully, because it preys upon the most primal parts of who we are. A traumatized human is easily controlled by the system; their lust is continuously exploited, and their life force energy is drained from their vessel by arousing images and provocative lyrics. Many of our artists and musicians have been completely compromised by the industry—their gifts have been commandeered and they've unknowingly become agents on the matrix. Pumping out tracks that keep us trapped in lower dimensions of reality.

In the Christian church, praise and worship music is used as a way of calling in the "Holy Ghost." From a scientific perspective, it is understood that certain frequencies of sound invoke entities or spirits—charges of energy dwelling within our bodies and all around us. Those in power are well aware of this information and have weaponized it against us, employing sound as a tool for oppression. Observe the music that's most marketed to certain demographics of people and you will begin to notice a pattern. It's not just entertainment. It's entrapment.

It is not just the beats that evoke these entities, but the lyrics. The "N-word," for example, which is used throughout popular music, although reclaimed in recent years, never truly belonged to us and it never will. There is no way of transmuting the energetic charge of what once was and still is actively being used as a racial slur. Our ancestors likely adopted the use of the N-word as a coping mechanism to soften the blow of hearing it daily from their oppressors. But using it is a bad habit normalized and fortified by time, just like consuming alcohol or smoking cigarettes. And just like those things, at its core this word is poisonous. This is something that I myself only recently have come into consciousness around and must actively practice eliminating from my vocabulary. As the creators of culture, we don't need the massah's hand-me-downs. Abandoning our use of the N-word isn't about adhering to standards of professionalism that are rooted in anti-Blackness. It is about returning to who we were as people prior to our abduction and relinquishing the programming we've taken on since.

* * *

Although I am deeply grateful for the less conscious version of myself who sacrificed her sacred vessel to build the platform upon which I stand today while navigating the limited opportunities for recognition that Black women are afforded in this matrix, in achieving higher levels of consciousness, I was forced to confront the ways I was perpetuating the energetic imprint of slavery in my occupation as a model by allowing my body to be used as a marketing tool to evoke lustful temptation from those who consumed images of me, quite literally consuming my life force energy. Like my mother, I was functioning within an energetic imprint that I had not yet excavated and eradicated from my body. Thus, I was subconsciously being used as a pawn to further the agenda of the higher-ups by glamorizing the exploitation of the Black woman's body under the guise of fashion and empowerment. We have to become critical of the ways that this glorification of sex, removed from its true spiritual essence, impacts our community. We must also become critical of the systems of oppression and economic conditions outside of the entertainment industry that perpetuate this issue. For centuries, Black women, and even men, have been systematically denied opportunities for economic advancement and, in many cases, have been forced to partake in sex work as a means of survival.

For the majority of descendants of enslaved people, without overlooking our incarcerated brothers and sisters, no longer is our bondage physical. Those devices have expired. The technology of the enemy has gotten so much more sophisticated, and we are now slaves to our minds and our carnal desires. Many of us choose to pick up our shackles and hold them in the palm of our hands daily. We are stuck in a never-ending circuit of imagery that triggers and plays upon our deepest collective wounds. And, without realizing it, we are constructing our reality based on that constant algorithmic intake of data. That is why social media sites and other applications have the potential to be so dangerous.

Hook-up apps, for example, have turned sex into a product, diminishing the significance of the act by reducing it to a left or right swipe. How is this any different from the commodification of our bodies while enslaved? When you could be looked up and down and it would be decided that you'd be forced into sexual encounters with a complete stranger? Except now we volunteer our bodies and our masters sit comfortably and silently on the other side of our subscriptions while reaping the benefits of our ongoing participation. And we play right into it. We perpetuate the system, overlooking the physical consequences and completely ignorant to the spiritual repercussions of our actions. We repeatedly open ourselves up to whatever low vibrating entities inhabit the vessels of those with whom we engage. Absorbing into our own psyche their addictions, their anxiety, their lust, and all other lower frequency emotions from past experiences, what Buddhists call "karma." For descendants of enslaved people, that karma is filled with centuries of pain.

There is no awareness of the psychological impact of taking on so much sexual energy, just a constant fixation on satisfying carnal desires and an endless cycle of pleasure followed by suppression that requires higher levels of perversion to meet previous levels of satisfaction. What we consume, therefore, begins to consume us. An input-output feedback loop of information is programmed into our psyche and is projected out into the world, shaping our primary experience. Until the feedback loop is disrupted with new choices, habits, or information, we live our lives in bondage to our own minds. Instead of programming our reality, we are allowing our reality to program us.

The illusion of freedom has only increased since slavery. What we are brainwashed to identify as liberation is quite literally the opposite. Social media essentially serves as a modern-day auction block, where we display the most intimate parts of ourselves for the world to see and judge. Brands, potential sponsors, and potential partners alike evaluate our worth through constant comparison to others to see whose is bigger and whose is better, and THIS determines our value. Black men feel inadequate if they can't afford and provide lavish lifestyles for themselves and their cohort of suitors, while Black women are dying on the operating table because they believe that augmenting their bodies in a way that evokes lust will allow them access to a lifestyle that they would otherwise be denied. We cosplay our own femininity while taking on the same pseudo-masculinity rooted in sexual conquest and violence that was once reserved for men, in reaction to the harm we have faced because of it. We do not recognize this as an issue, because we have been programmed to believe the roles that are traditionally feminine make us weak. And within the context of society today, with capitalism as the driving force upon which our survival depends, they do. But, rather than condemning the system, we have adapted to it. In reality, to be responsible for the wellness of your family is a position of authority unmatched by any other, and as African and Indigenous women we knew this.

It was European colonialists that made servants out of their wives and relegated them to a lower status in the home, which ultimately led to their unrest. African women were not just made to cook, clean, and rear children; they were women of commerce and trade who did meaningful work that benefited themselves and their communities. They were healers and spiritualists, who knew that their knowledge held the capacity to determine the longevity and prosperity of their kin. Above all, they were submissive, not to man but to nature. They had no need to hustle and keep up with the demands of the world, because they knew that true provision came from their unfailing connection to the earth.

So how do we return to who we were prior to our abduction? How do we restore our innocence? We do it by once more becoming childlike and returning ourselves to the source, to nature . . . our eternal mother. We once more understand our connection to earth as our ancestors understood it and, as if reentering our mothers' wombs, we reattach ourselves to her umbilical cord, which supplies us an unyielding abundance of sustenance. We once more recognize ourselves as a part of an ecosystem, realizing that there is no liberation for humanity without the liberation of the planet, and there is no liberation for the planet without the liberation of humanity, for we are inextricably linked. Everything that has been done to our bodies—rape, pillage, and conquest—has also been done to her.

We must come to understand that all matter begins as energy, and what we experience as physical reality is merely a projection of the state of our collective consciousness. If we wish to collapse the systems of oppression that binds us, it must be done not through protest or externalized outrage but from within. We do not need to fight the system but to starve it of our energy. We must become conscious of the ways this Western matrix shows up in our own behavior and thought forms. We must closely monitor our consumption of all things, from food to music, and examine the methods by which our energy is siphoned and used to entrench us in even deeper layers of oppression.

Are you using your vessel and sexual energy with full agency and autonomy, or are you using it to garner attention and solicit lust? Are you using it to serve your highest purpose, or to provoke a reaction from those who consume your content? Are you exposing the most intimate parts of yourself in hopes that it will lead to the acquisition of wealth, worldly possessions, and proximity to certain people? These are the questions we must begin to ask ourselves.

We can no longer forfeit our autonomy and place our collective well-being in the hands of elected officials and those we view as having more power than us. There is no candidate more qualified to improve the quality of your life than you. Forget what is popular and what has become normalized by society. The forces of evil are strong and have misled many. It is crucial that we look not outside of ourselves for guidance but within. We must take inventory of our existence and reclaim our sovereignty by renegotiating our participation in the system. How are your daily choices upholding and perpetuating it? Are you living authentically or conforming to the expectations of others? Are your habits and behaviors the result of you consciously choosing them or a product of your environment, upbringing, and conditioning? Are you allowing those in your life who drain you of your energy to occupy space? Are you eating foods that support your body or slow it down? Are you being distracted and emotionally manipulated by what's going on in the media? Where are you placing your focus?

In 2023, the revolution is not black leather jackets, berets, and rifles as it was in the '70s. It is not yelling into megaphones and marching in the streets, although that certainly has its place. The revolution is silent, internal, and individual. The revolution is choosing ourselves, our truth, and our wellness over everything else with conscious humility. If you are merely addressing society's ills based on the physical constructs that oppress us, you have no idea the size of the monster you are up against. We are all on a sacred spiritual journey. Some of us belly to the ground, others of us wings to the sky. But regardless of our current position, we have been called by the universe, not in yells but in whispers, to become more aware in this moment than we have ever been. This is inter-dimensional warfare, your weapons are discipline and accountability, and the cost is your soul.

Are you listening?

Have you tuned in to your calling?

Are you ready to fight?

Butterfly

In this existence we dwell suspended in duality—in every instant we
    are both the caterpillar and the butterfly

The caterpillar's vision is eclipsed by her own judgment

The caterpillar envies the butterfly, unaware of her own potential f
    or flight

Chrysalises begin to form in her mind, eventually shaping the world
    around her

Encapsulating her, suffocating her

It is her own ignorance that keeps her blind

Keeps her blind to her infinite potential

Keeps her blind to the world

Keeps her blind to possibility

Ignorance of her true self

Ignorance of others

Ignorance of what lies beyond her immediate circumstances

She cannot see her way out

She only knows darkness

She is dying

But this is not death

It is rebirth

It is evolution

It is only through this darkness and solitude that she is finally able
    to understand

To truly become free, the caterpillar must forfeit all ideas of who she
    thought she was

All ideas of who the world told her she was
She surrenders to her greatness
She surrenders to her destiny
She is transformed
The butterfly becomes aware of the chrysalis and knows she must
    break out
Shedding the protective layers that once encased her
They won't serve her in this new life
They only weigh her down
The butterfly is liberated by the newfound truth of who she is
Liberated by her newfound perspective
The butterfly does not judge the caterpillar for her lack of awareness
Or for what the caterpillar did not know
The butterfly is not ashamed of her inglorious past
She gives thanks to the caterpillar for her resilience
For bringing her to this point in the journey
You see, my dear, the caterpillar was always the butterfly
Her great metamorphosis is the product of the suffering she
    overcame
The caterpillar was born knowing how to fly
She just needed to remember her wings
It was through adversity that she was reminded
The butterfly, although joyously free from her mistaken identity,
Loves the caterpillar unconditionally
They are one and the same
Living eternally in divine union

About the Author

Ebonee Davis is an American model, poet, actor, and activist from Seattle, Washington.

Since beginning her career in 2012, Ebonee has become one of the fashion industry's most prominent voices, advocating for representation and diversity in front of the camera as well as behind it. In 2017, Ebonee was asked to give a TED Talk at the University of Nevada on the topic of systemic bias in fashion, which she titled "Black Girl Magic in the Fashion Industry."

She has since appeared on numerous covers and in publications such as *Vogue*, *Harper's Bazaar*, *Essence*, and *CRWN*.

In 2019, Ebonee founded Daughter Org, her nonprofit educational organization dedicated to unifying children of the diaspora by returning to West Africa for immersive birthright experiences.

Ebonee currently resides in Atlanta, Georgia.